No-Bake Desserts

DO NOT SHELVE

This book is
property of the

MINEOLA

MEMORIAL

LIBRARY

Also by Addie Gundry

Family Favorite Casserole Recipes:
103 Comforting Breakfast Casseroles, Dinner Ideas,
and Desserts Everyone Will Love

No-Bake Desserts

103 Easy Recipes for No-Bake
Cookies, Bars, and Treats

Addie Gundry

St. Martin's Griffin ✹ New York

NO-BAKE DESSERTS. Copyright © 2017 by Addie Gundry. All rights reserved. Printed in the United States of America. For information, address St. Martin's Press, 175 Fifth Avenue, New York, N.Y. 10010.

www.stmartins.com

Photographs © 2017 by Megan Von Schönoff

The Library of Congress Cataloging-in-Publication Data is available upon request.

ISBN 978-1-250-12336-7 (trade paperback)
ISBN 978-1-250-12337-4 (e-book)

Our books may be purchased in bulk for promotional, educational, or business use. Please contact your local bookseller or the Macmillan Corporate and Premium Sales Department at 1-800-221-7945, extension 5442, or by e-mail at MacmillanSpecialMarkets@macmillan.com.

First Edition: June 2017

10 9 8 7 6 5 4 3 2 1

To Miss Porter's School, a magical place.
Thank you for instilling in me a brave sense of
confidence, teaching me independence and kindness,
and, most important, for giving me sisters.

Contents

3
Cookies, Bites, and Bars

4
Fruit and Frozen Desserts

5
Gelatin and Pudding Desserts

6
Desserts in a Jar

No-Bake Desserts

Introduction

I went to an all-girls boarding school. You might imagine crisp, plaid uniforms; books balanced on top of heads; and single-file lines around every corner, but it wasn't like that at all. It was at Miss Porter's, in AP Physics, that I learned how to fly a paper airplane. It was there that I discovered my favorite book, *The Great Gatsby*, and proceeded to read it over and over in my free time. I played sports all three seasons, spent a majority of my time muddy, and none of my clothes were ironed. It was there that I learned what a party really was.

At the time I didn't know how to cook very well, nor did we have ovens to cook in, but I began reading about food. I ripped out magazine articles to study why ingredients worked together, and why cooking times and temperatures could make or break a recipe. I found that without an oven I still could not be stopped, and thus my love for semi-homemade, no-bake desserts came to be. I learned that if I wanted to throw parties for a living and fill a table with beautiful food, I could. I learned how to learn, why a work ethic and education were important, and that allowed me to study and pursue a career in something I was passionate about. It may have been confusing to my American History and French teachers, but fast-forward a few years, and I was formally trained in the culinary arts.

Back then, and still today, it wasn't about the color coordinating, or the décor hanging high, the picture-perfect moments we share on social media. It's about the people who surround the table, like those girls from Miss Porter's. It was, and still is, about the company and conversation, and the good food (no matter if some was store-bought). I've used my experience and excitement for food and entertaining to create each one of the 103 no-bake desserts in a unique way. Why 103? When you come to our house for dinner or dessert, we want you to know you can always bring a friend, or two, or three . . . and for those who have been to our home, you know firsthand that guests tend to multiply as the food continues to come out of the oven and cocktails are poured. One hundred recipes felt too rigid, so finite, and so by adding the extra three it became more welcoming—a reminder that there is always more room at the table.

As the ice cream became a melty mess on a hot weekend at home in June, more guests arrived, making the last-minute sticky situation a fun one. Strawberries were buy-one-get-one-free, and you better believe the Chocolate Mousse (page 173) I make now is far less temperamental than the recipe I learned in culinary school in France. When I melted chocolate to make Rainbow Mint Bark (page 60), I had a lot of pretzels and with a little extra white chocolate, a few got covered until smothered by sticky fingers and excited friends. Those vanilla cookies, that I did not bake, were turned into Vanilla Cookie Sandwiches (page 109), and the Almond Brittle (page 76) is probably the most sophisticated item on the menu—that, and the prosecco. On the flip side, the Mint Chocolate

Chip Cups (page 200) are made with store-bought pudding, so although elegant, they remain easy. A perfect party isn't perfect. That's what makes it a party. In the end, you won't remember the lit-tle things that didn't go quite as smoothly as you hoped. But you will remember that it was a great party, and that is what is important.

—Addie Gundry

1

Cakes and Pies

As Julia Child once said, "A party without a cake is just a meeting." I happen to agree. In this chapter you will find cheesecakes, beautiful pies, fruit tarts, and more—all with the magical ability to turn any day into a party.

Brownie Cheesecake

Yield: 1 cake; serves 10 to 12 | Prep Time: 1 hour | Chill Time: 1 to 2 hours

When I was a kid visiting family in Chicago, the highlight of the experience was always getting to dine at my favorite restaurant, The Cheesecake Factory. With so many cheesecakes to choose from, I was always happy to share, so I could try multiple flavors. One of my favorites was a brownie cheesecake because it was a mash-up of two great desserts. This one isn't quite as giant as the cheesecake I ate on the first floor of the Hancock building, but it equally delicious.

INGREDIENTS

2 dozen brownie bites

1½ cups bittersweet chocolate chips

12 ounces cream cheese, at room temperature

4 tablespoons (½ stick/ ¼ cup) unsalted butter, softened

½ teaspoon instant espresso powder

½ cup granulated sugar

1 cup cold heavy whipping cream

2 tablespoons powdered sugar

¾ cup mini chocolate chips, plus additional for serving

1 (12.25-ounce) jar store-bought sea salt–caramel sauce

DIRECTIONS

1. Lightly grease an 8-inch springform pan.

2. Arrange the brownie bites to fit in the bottom of the pan.

3. In a medium microwave-safe bowl, microwave the bittersweet chocolate chips on high for 1 minute. Stir and continue to microwave in 30-second intervals until the chocolate has melted, about 3 minutes total. Set aside to cool while you prepare the cream cheese.

4. Using a hand mixer and a large bowl, or in the bowl of a stand mixer fitted with the paddle, beat the cream cheese, butter, espresso powder, and granulated sugar on medium speed until smooth.

5. Add the cooled melted chocolate and beat on medium speed until combined.

6. Mix the heavy whipping cream with the powdered sugar until stiff peaks form.

7. Fold the whipped cream into the cream cheese mixture. Add ¾ cup of the mini chocolate chips.

8. Spoon the batter into the pan over the brownies.

9. Refrigerate for 1 to 2 hours, until firm.

10. Remove the springform ring from the cheesecake.

11. Warm the sea salt–caramel sauce. Drizzle a few tablespoons over the cheesecake and top with the remaining mini chocolate chips. Serve immediately.

Chocolate Éclair Cake

Yield: 1 cake; serves 8 to 10 | Prep Time: 15 minutes | Chill Time: Overnight

This delicious, slightly messy, sticky cake is well worth the overnight wait. With the multi-dimensional layers, it looks complex but is very simple to create and a showstopper for any party.

INGREDIENTS

2 (3.5-ounce) packages instant vanilla pudding mix

3 cups plus 1 tablespoon whole milk

1 (8-ounce) container frozen whipped topping, thawed

1 (14.4-ounce) box graham crackers

⅓ cup Nutella

1 tablespoon corn syrup

DIRECTIONS

1. In a medium bowl, combine the pudding mix and 3 cups of the milk. Add the whipped topping and stir to combine.

2. Place one layer of graham crackers on the bottom of a 9 × 13-inch baking dish. Top with the pudding–whipped topping mixture and repeat with an additional layer of graham crackers and pudding–whipped topping mixture. End with a layer of graham crackers.

3. In a small microwave-safe bowl, combine the Nutella and the remaining 1 tablespoon milk and melt in the microwave on medium heat for 20 seconds. Stir in the corn syrup.

4. Pour the Nutella mixture on top of the cake. Refrigerate overnight.

5. Cut into slices and serve.

Mocha Chocolate Icebox Cake

Yield: 1 cake; serves 8 to 10 | Prep Time: 20 minutes | Chill Time: 3 hours

My fondest memories of my grandmother are her morning cups of coffee and her long list of icebox desserts that she'd turn to each week in the summer. When I eventually began drinking coffee, both the smell and taste brought back these memories. I don't know if I remember her combining that morning coffee into any of her icebox cakes, but if she did, it would be exactly this cake.

INGREDIENTS

1 (9-ounce) package chocolate wafer cookies

3 tablespoons whole milk

3 tablespoons instant espresso powder

3½ cups cold heavy whipping cream

1 teaspoon vanilla extract

1¼ cups powdered sugar

12 ounces cream cheese, at room temperature

¾ cup granulated sugar

12 ounces chocolate chips or melting chocolate wafers

DIRECTIONS

1. Crush the cookies in a food processor to the consistency of wet sand.

2. In a small saucepan, heat the milk until it begins to steam. Stir in the espresso powder and set aside to steep.

3. In the bowl of a stand mixer fitted with the wire whip, whip 2½ cups of the heavy whipping cream on high until foamy. Add the vanilla and powdered sugar and continue whipping until stiff peaks form. Transfer to a large bowl and set aside.

4. In the same mixer bowl (no need to wash) using the paddle attachment, combine the cream cheese and granulated sugar and mix for 2 minutes, scraping down the sides of the bowl, until smooth. Add the espresso-milk mixture and stir to incorporate. Fold the two mixtures together until no white streaks remain. Place in the refrigerator to chill.

5. Meanwhile, put the chocolate chips in a large bowl. Heat the remaining 1 cup heavy whipping cream in a small saucepan over medium heat until steamy. Pour the cream over the chips and stir until a smooth, shiny ganache forms.

6. Place half the crumbs into a greased 8-inch springform pan and press with your fingertips to form a bottom crust. Spoon in half the whipped filling and smooth. Pour ½ cup of the ganache over the filling and carefully smooth. Repeat the layering.

7. Chill the cake for at least 3 hours before serving.

Mug Cake

Yield: 1 individual mug cake | Prep Time: 5 minutes | Cook Time: 1 minute

It may be hard to believe that you can make a cake without an oven and in only 60 seconds, but it's true. If you have the ingredients in your office, then that breakroom microwave will be kept in continuous use.

INGREDIENTS

¼ cup all-purpose flour

2 tablespoons unsweetened cocoa powder

¼ teaspoon baking powder

3 tablespoons sugar

¼ cup whole milk

3 tablespoons vegetable oil

Malted milk balls, cut or crushed, for topping

Store-bought chocolate sauce, for topping

DIRECTIONS

1. In a small bowl, combine the flour, cocoa powder, baking powder, and sugar.

2. Add the milk and vegetable oil and stir well to incorporate.

3. Pour the batter into a large mug.

4. Microwave on high for 60 seconds. Remove from the microwave and top with malted milk balls and chocolate sauce.

NOTE

All microwaves are different. You may need more time for your cake to cook. After 60 seconds, check the cake and place back in the microwave if it is not doughy and solid. There are no eggs to worry about undercooking, so if it is a bit gooey, that is OK, too!

No-Bake Nutella Cheesecake

Yield: 6 mini cheesecakes | Prep Time: 15 minutes | Chill Time: 4 hours

Nutella has a distinct taste and texture unlike any other chocolate product I can think of. So you don't need to add much to make a delicious chocolate-hazelnut-flavored cheesecake. This simple, sweet little treat will taste exactly as it's named.

INGREDIENTS

1 (13-ounce) jar Nutella

2 (8-ounce) packages cream cheese, at room temperature

½ cup powdered sugar

6 store-bought mini graham cracker pie crusts

1 cup white chocolate chips

1 cup bittersweet chocolate chips

DIRECTIONS

1. In the bowl of a stand mixer fitted with the paddle, beat the Nutella, cream cheese, and powdered sugar on medium speed until smooth and combined.

2. Spoon the mixture into the graham cracker crusts.

3. In a small microwave-safe bowl, microwave the white chocolate chips on 50% power in 30-second increments until the chocolate has completely melted.

4. Drizzle the cheesecakes with the white chocolate and top with the bittersweet chocolate chips. Refrigerate for at least 4 hours before serving.

Pineapple Dream Cake

Yield: 1 cake; serves 8 to 10 | Prep Time: 15 minutes | Chill Time: Overnight

This sweet little treat reminds me of a menu item at a tiki bar, and I can certainly imagine eating a big slice on the beach or by the pool. A similar color to the sea of big yellow umbrellas that sprawl across the sand, this easy cake is truly a vacation in a pan.

INGREDIENTS

1 (11-ounce) box mini vanilla wafers

1 (20-ounce) can crushed pineapple

½ cup lemon juice

1 (14-ounce) can sweetened condensed milk

1 (8-ounce) container frozen whipped topping, thawed

1 (7-ounce) package sweetened flaked coconut

Maraschino cherries for garnish

DIRECTIONS

1. Place a solid layer of vanilla wafer cookies on the bottom of an 8- or 9-inch square deep-dish pan.

2. In a small bowl, combine the pineapple, lemon juice, and condensed milk. Pour the mixture on top of the vanilla wafers in the pan.

3. Place more wafers on top and then cover with the whipped topping and the coconut.

4. Refrigerate the cake overnight.

5. To serve, scoop into individual serving dishes and top each with a cherry.

No-Bake Balsamic Berry Cheesecake

Yield: 1 cheesecake; serves 8 to 10 | Prep Time: 15 minutes | Chill Time: 5 hours or overnight

Plain cheesecakes are completely delicious as is, but they're also the perfect canvas for all kinds of toppings and fillings. In the summer, fresh berries are in abundance, and topping a slice with as many as possible makes this savory-sweet treat even better. What I love to do with cheesecakes is add something slightly tangy. It cuts into the thick and rich filling and provides a sauce.

INGREDIENTS

2 (8-ounce) packages cream cheese, at room temperature

1 teaspoon vanilla extract

1 cup powdered sugar

½ cup sour cream

¾ cup cold heavy whipping cream

1 store-bought (or homemade) graham cracker pie crust

Sauce

1 cup mixed fresh berries (strawberries, blueberries, and blackberries), plus extra for serving

¼ cup balsamic vinegar

¼ cup granulated sugar

1 tablespoon lemon juice

DIRECTIONS

1. In the bowl of a stand mixer fitted with the paddle, combine the cream cheese, vanilla, and powdered sugar and beat until smooth. Add the sour cream and heavy whipping cream and beat until thick and creamy, about 5 minutes.

2. Pour the filling into the graham cracker crust and refrigerate the cheesecake for at least 5 hours or overnight.

Sauce

3. When ready to serve, make the berry sauce. In a small saucepan, combine the fresh berries, vinegar, granulated sugar, and lemon juice. Cook over medium heat, stirring, until the sugar dissolves, about 5 minutes.

4. Set the sauce aside to cool for a few minutes.

5. To serve, slice the cake, place on individual serving plates, and drizzle with the sauce. Top with extra berries.

No-Bake Cherry Cheesecake Bites

Yield: 12 mini cheesecake bites | Prep Time: 15 minutes | Chill Time: 4 hours

I love these little bites because they are great for kids and adults. They also happen to be my go-to convenience treat for parties; something a little less sweet and perfect for passing around, navigating through a crowd, and eating one handed, leaving your other hand free for a cocktail.

INGREDIENTS

1 cup graham cracker crumbs

4 tablespoons (½ stick / ¼ cup) unsalted butter, melted

1 (8-ounce) package cream cheese, at room temperature

1 (14-ounce) can sweetened condensed milk

⅓ cup lemon juice

1 teaspoon vanilla extract

Pinch of kosher salt

1 (20-ounce) can cherry pie filling

Maraschino cherries, for serving

DIRECTIONS

1. Line a mini cupcake tin with paper liners.

2. In a small bowl, mix the graham cracker crumbs and melted butter together. Press into the bottom of the lined cups with a spoon. Refrigerate for 1 hour.

3. In the bowl of a stand mixer fitted with the paddle, beat the cream cheese until light and fluffy. Gradually add the sweetened condensed milk and beat until well combined. Stir in the lemon juice, vanilla, and salt.

4. Pour the mixture into the prepared crusts and chill the cheesecakes for 3 hours.

5. Top with the cherry pie filling and maraschino cherries. Serve immediately.

Chocolate-Raspberry Cheesecake

Yield: 1 cheesecake; serves 10 to 12 | Prep Time: 15 minutes | Chill Time: 4 hours

I've served this showstopper in the summer with fresh-picked berries and over Christmastime with a little holly on the plate. It's a year-round beauty. The dark chocolate crust paired with the bright pink cake is elegant and striking on any table.

INGREDIENTS

1 (8-ounce) package cream cheese, at room temperature

1 (8-ounce) container frozen whipped topping, thawed

2 teaspoons blue raspberry Jell-O powder

2 cups raspberry preserves

1½ cups powdered sugar

1 store-bought (or homemade) chocolate cookie crust

1 pint fresh raspberries

DIRECTIONS

1. In the bowl of a stand mixer fitted with the paddle, combine the cream cheese, whipped topping, and Jell-O powder. Mix on high until well blended, about 5 minutes.

2. Add the raspberry preserves and powdered sugar.

3. Pour the filling into the prepared chocolate crust and top with the fresh raspberries.

4. Refrigerate the pie for 4 hours. Serve chilled.

NOTE

The Jell-O provides color and flavor, making it one of my favorite double-agent secret ingredients!

Nutter Butter Cheesecake

Yield: 1 cheesecake; serves 10 to 12 | Prep Time: 1 hour | Chill Time: 5 hours or overnight

Nutter Butter cookies make the perfect cheesecake crusts. The peanut butter binds the cookie crumbs together, and when packed in tightly, the mixture forms a thick, sturdy base for the light and fluffy topping.

INGREDIENTS

Crust

24 Nutter Butter cookies

1 tablespoon granulated sugar

4–5 tablespoons unsalted butter, melted

Filling

2 (8-ounce) packages cream cheese, at room temperature

1 cup creamy peanut butter

1 cup granulated sugar

16 ounces cold heavy whipping cream

¼ cup powdered sugar

1 teaspoon vanilla extract

8 Nutter Butter cookies, broken

2 (8-ounce) containers frozen whipped topping, thawed, for garnish

Mini marshmallows for garnish

DIRECTIONS

Crust

1. To make the crust, crush the cookies in the food processor until finely crushed. Add the granulated sugar and melted butter.

2. Press the mixture into the bottom and up the sides of a 9-inch springform pan.

3. Refrigerate for 1 hour, until firm.

Filling

4. In the bowl of a stand mixer fitted with the paddle, beat the cream cheese, peanut butter, and granulated sugar until well combined.

5. In a clean mixer bowl fitted with the wire whip, whip the cream, powdered sugar, and vanilla until firm peaks form.

6. Fold the whipped cream mixture into the cream cheese–peanut butter mixture. Fold in the broken cookies.

7. Spread the mixture over the crust.

8. Refrigerate the cheesecake for at least 4 hours or overnight.

9. Serve, garnished with whipped topping, mini marshmallows, and extra crushed Nutter Butter cookies.

Strawberry-Raspberry Fluff Cake

Yield: 1 cake; serves 6 to 8 | Prep Time: 15 minutes | Chill Time: Overnight

The other day I brought this cake to a baby shower. It's a sweet little treat perfect for a girly occasion: as light as air and as fluffy as a cloud, just like it looks.

INGREDIENTS

1 (8-ounce) package cream cheese, at room temperature

1 (8-ounce) container frozen whipped topping, thawed

2 teaspoons blue raspberry Jell-O powder

1 cup strawberry preserves

1½ cups powdered sugar

1 store-bought (or homemade) graham cracker crust

Chopped strawberries for garnish

DIRECTIONS

1. In the bowl of a stand mixer fitted with the paddle, combine the cream cheese, whipped topping, and Jell-O powder.

2. Mix on high until well blended and the Jell-O powder has dissolved, about 5 minutes.

3. Add the strawberry preserves and powdered sugar and beat until fully incorporated.

4. Pour the filling into the graham cracker crust and refrigerate the cake overnight.

5. Top with chopped strawberries and serve.

Chocolate Chip Cookie Pie

Yield: 1 pie; serves 6 to 8 | Prep Time: 15 minutes | Chill Time: 8 hours or overnight

This pie tastes like my childhood memories of dipping chocolate chip cookies into milk at night. That's one of those activities that as you get older feels more indulgent than anything. But right now, I give you permission to dunk cookies in milk for as long as you live! As the cookies absorb the whipped topping, they assume the milk-soaked taste of my favorite bedtime snack.

INGREDIENTS

1 (13-ounce) package chocolate chip cookies

2 cups heavy whipping cream

1 store-bought (or homemade) graham cracker crust

2 (8-ounce) containers frozen whipped topping, thawed

DIRECTIONS

1. Dip the cookies into the heavy whipping cream and place in a layer on the bottom of the graham cracker crust.

2. Top with half (1 container) of the whipped topping.

3. Add another layer of cookies that have been dipped in cream, and top with more whipped topping.

4. Repeat for a third time.

5. Crush up the remaining cookies and top the cookie pie.

6. Chill the pie for 8 hours or overnight.

7. Serve chilled.

Chocolate-Strawberry Pie

Yield: 1 pie; serves 6 to 8 | Prep Time: 15 minutes | Chill Time: 2 hours

This is a fun and unique way to make an elegant chocolate dessert in only 15 minutes! Strawberries may be the most popular berry out there, and come summer when their season is in full swing, you can't get anything sweeter! I love tasting the delicious berries as they combine with the rich chocolate and crunchy crust.

INGREDIENTS

1 pint fresh strawberries, washed, trimmed, and halved

1 store-bought (or homemade) chocolate cookie pie crust

⅔ cup sugar

¼ cup cornstarch

2 tablespoons unsweetened cocoa powder

¼ teaspoon minced crystallized ginger

⅛ teaspoon ground nutmeg

Pinch of kosher or sea salt

6 large egg yolks

2½ cups half-and-half

6 ounces bittersweet or semisweet chocolate, chopped

½ tablespoon rum extract

1 teaspoon vanilla extract

Additional strawberries for garnish (optional)

DIRECTIONS

1. Place the strawberry halves in a single layer in the bottom of the pie crust.

2. In a medium saucepan, whisk together the sugar, cornstarch, cocoa powder, ginger, nutmeg, and salt over medium heat.

3. Whisk in the egg yolks to create a thick paste. Gradually whisk in the half-and-half until the mixture thickens, about 5 minutes. Bring to a boil and cook for 1 minute. Remove from the heat.

4. Add the chocolate and whisk until combined. Add the rum and vanilla extracts. Cool the mixture for 5 minutes.

5. Pour the filling over the strawberries and up to the top of the crust. Chill the pie for 2 hours or until set.

6. Garnish with additional strawberries, if desired.

Coconut Cream Pie

Yield: 1 pie; serves 6 to 8 | Prep Time: 15 minutes | Chill Time: 2 to 3 hours

I love coconut: desserts, candies, even coconut-infused savory dishes like chicken and rice. My husband, on the other hand, not so much. So when I make coconut cream pie, I always make it when he is out of town for business and invite my girlfriends over to share while we watch our favorite shows.

INGREDIENTS

1 (5.1-ounce) package (or two 3.4-ounce packages) instant vanilla pudding mix

2 cups whole milk

1 teaspoon coconut extract

1 (8-ounce) container frozen whipped topping, thawed

¾ cup sweetened flaked coconut

1 store-bought (or homemade) chocolate cookie pie crust

Sweetened flaked coconut, silver sugar pearls, and sliced bananas for garnish (optional)

DIRECTIONS

1. In a large bowl, beat the pudding mix, milk, and coconut extract with a whisk for 2 minutes until smooth. Slowly mix in the whipped topping and flaked coconut.

2. Pour the filling into the prepared crust and sprinkle with the flaked coconut, silver sugar pearls, and banana slices, if desired.

3. Chill the pie for 2 to 3 hours.

4. Serve chilled.

VARIATION

Or use mini prepared pie crusts.

French Silk Pie

Yield: 1 pie; serves 6 to 8 | Prep Time: 20 minutes | Chill Time: 1 hour

Pretzels are my favorite food, so I can't help sneaking them into even the most unexpected recipes. While not a traditional take on a French Silk Pie with pastry tart crust, this version is just as decadent, and I hope you love the surprising change—a salty pretzel crust.

INGREDIENTS

Pretzel Crust

8 tablespoons (1 stick / ½ cup) unsalted butter, melted

¼ cup honey

1¾ cups crushed salted pretzels

Filling

8 tablespoons (1 stick / ½ cup) unsalted butter, softened

1½ cups powdered sugar

½ cup semisweet chocolate chips, melted

Pinch of kosher salt

2 teaspoons vanilla extract

2 tablespoons sour cream

1 teaspoon instant espresso powder

Whipped topping for garnish

DIRECTIONS

Pretzel Crust

1. Grease an 8- or 9-inch pie plate or springform pan.

2. In a bowl, mix together the melted butter and honey until smooth. Add the crushed pretzels and mix until combined. Press the mixture firmly against the bottom and sides of the greased pie plate or springform pan. Transfer to the fridge to chill.

Filling

3. Meanwhile, make the filling. Using an electric mixer and a large bowl, cream together the butter and powdered sugar until light and fluffy, about 3 minutes.

4. Add the melted chocolate, salt, vanilla, sour cream, and espresso powder and mix until combined and smooth.

5. Pour the filling into the chilled pie crust, and return it to the fridge for at least 1 hour.

6. Serve, topped with whipped topping.

Key Lime Pie

Yield: 1 pie; serves 6 to 8 | Prep Time: 15 minutes | Chill Time: 1 hour

Key lime pie is one of the greatest inventions. You can't go wrong with tart lime juice combined with thick sweetened condensed milk—the combination is just too good. This take on the key lime pie, with Greek yogurt, adds a little more of that tang and is as delicious as can be.

INGREDIENTS

1 (8-ounce) package cream cheese, at room temperature

½ cup nonfat vanilla Greek yogurt

½ (14-ounce) can sweetened condensed milk

⅓ cup key lime juice (see Note)

Green food coloring (optional)

1 store-bought (or homemade) graham cracker crust

Whipped topping for serving

Key limes for garnish, zested and sliced

DIRECTIONS

1. In the bowl of a stand mixer fitted with the paddle, combine the cream cheese, yogurt, condensed milk, and lime juice. Mix well until smooth. Add a drop of green food coloring if desired.

2. Pour the key lime mixture into the crust and chill the pie for 1 hour.

3. Top with whipped topping and garnish with lime zest and slices of lime. Serve immediately.

NOTE

If you can't find key limes, don't worry; use regular limes, they taste just as amazing.

Multicolor Kool-Aid Pie

Yield: 1 pie; serves 6 to 8 | Prep Time: 10 minutes | Chill Time: 4 hours or overnight

Ombré, when one color fades into another, is a trend that has taken hold of everything from fashion to hair color and even wedding cakes. I happen to think it's beautiful, like an elegant version of tie-dye. When I found ombré doilies at the store, I had to make a pie that mimicked something similar. Colored with blue raspberry and black cherry, this pie is as pretty as it is tasty.

INGREDIENTS

1 (14-ounce) can sweetened condensed milk

2 (8-ounce) containers frozen whipped topping, thawed, plus extra for garnish

1 (0.14-ounce) packet of blue raspberry Kool-Aid

1 (0.14-ounce) packet black cherry Kool-Aid

1 store-bought (or homemade) graham cracker crust

Silver sugar pearls for garnish

DIRECTIONS

1. In a medium bowl, combine the sweetened condensed milk and 1 container of the whipped topping.

2. Add the two packets of Kool-Aid and stir until the colors begin to marble, without completely coloring the batter.

3. Pour into the graham cracker crust.

4. Top with the remaining whipped topping and transfer to the freezer. Freeze the pie for at least 4 hours, or overnight.

5. Top with additional whipped topping and silver sugar pearls. Serve cold.

Millionaire Pie

Yield: 1 pie; serves 6 to 8 | Prep Time: 10 to 15 minutes | Chill Time: 3 hours or overnight

Originally a Southern belle, this pie from South Carolina was so rich and delicious, it easily coined the name "Millionaire Pie." I think it is the deliciousness, and the sweet nature and strong structure of this dessert that make it so worthy of the name.

INGREDIENTS

1 cup sweetened flaked coconut

1 (15.25-ounce) can crushed pineapple, drained

1 cup maraschino cherries, stemmed, drained, and chopped

½ cup chopped walnuts

1 (14-ounce) can sweetened condensed milk

⅓ cup lemon juice

1 tablespoon maraschino cherry juice

½ teaspoon coconut extract

1 cup freshly whipped heavy cream, plus extra for serving

4 ounces mascarpone cheese, at room temperature

1 store-bought (or homemade) graham cracker crust

Whole maraschino cherries, pecans, sweetened flaked coconut, pineapple, silver sugar pearls for garnish

DIRECTIONS

1. In a large bowl, combine the flaked coconut, pineapple, maraschino cherries, walnuts, condensed milk, lemon juice, cherry juice, and coconut extract.

2. Whisk together the whipped cream and mascarpone cheese until combined and smooth.

3. Gently fold the whipped cream–mascarpone mixture into the coconut mixture.

4. Spread the mixture into the crust.

5. Refrigerate the pie for 3 hours or overnight.

6. Top with the garnishes and serve.

VARIATION

Or use mini prepared pie crusts.

Rainbow Pie

Yield: 1 pie; serves 6 to 8 | Prep Time: 10 minutes | Chill Time: 4 hours or overnight

I think this is what unicorns eat. As they are immortal, can scale walls, adapt to water living, heal animals, talk, and most importantly—sparkle—this pie seems like a dish that would improve each one of those powers for all who enjoy its deliciously colorful goodness.

INGREDIENTS

1 (14-ounce) can sweetened condensed milk

6 tablespoons lemon juice

½ teaspoon coconut extract

1 (14-ounce) can crushed pineapple, drained

½ cup sweetened flaked coconut

1 cup thawed whipped topping, plus extra for serving

3½ cups fruit-flavored mini or large marshmallows

1 store-bought (or homemade) graham cracker pie crust

Pineapple slices, sweetened flaked coconut, and mini marshmallows for garnish (optional)

DIRECTIONS

1. In a large bowl, whisk together the condensed milk, lemon juice, and coconut extract.

2. Fold in the crushed pineapple, flaked coconut, whipped topping, and marshmallows.

3. Pile the filling into the crust. Refrigerate the pie for 4 hours or overnight.

4. Garnish with pineapple slices, sweetened flaked coconut, and mini marshmallows, if desired.

Strawberry Pie

Yield: 1 pie; serves 6 to 8 | Prep Time: 15 minutes | Chill Time: Overnight

What I love about fruity desserts is that they can naturally be bright pink! This reminds me of strawberry ice cream with its buttery thick texture and hunks of ripe berries hiding inside. With a little whipped cream and graham cracker crust, a slice or two is the cure to any blues on a hot summer day.

INGREDIENTS

1 (3.4-ounce) package strawberry Jell-O

2 (8-ounce) containers frozen whipped topping, thawed

1 pint fresh strawberries, washed, hulled, and sliced

1 store-bought (or homemade) graham cracker pie crust

DIRECTIONS

1. Make the Jell-O according to the package directions.

2. Combine the Jell-O with 1 container of the whipped topping.

3. Add three-quarters of the strawberries.

4. Pour the mixture into the crust and chill the pie in the refrigerator overnight.

5. Serve, garnished with the remaining whipped topping and the remaining fresh strawberry slices.

2

Candies and Chocolates

Candy happens to be my favorite food group. From rock candy
to dipped pretzels, chocolate hearts to champagne gummies,
you won't need to walk down the candy aisle when this chapter
gives you everything you need to create one in your home.

Dipped Pretzels

Yield: 30 dipped pretzels | Prep Time: 5 minutes | Chill Time: 15 minutes

I love making dipped pretzels at home because I can color and sprinkle them any way that I want. I made these with decorative sugars that I had in my pantry and have also made them for Halloween (with black and orange), Christmas (with red and green), and Valentine's Day (with tiny hearts). The options are endless.

INGREDIENTS

8 ounces white or dark chocolate melting chocolate wafers

30 pretzels

Sprinkles, chopped nuts, toffee bits, drizzle of colored melted chocolate

DIRECTIONS

1. Line a baking sheet with parchment paper.

2. Melt the chocolate according to the package directions.

3. Dip the pretzels into the chocolate and place on the baking sheet.

4. Before the chocolate sets, sprinkle with sprinkles, nuts, etc.

5. Let dry at room temperature, or transfer to the fridge to set more quickly, before serving.

Walnut Fudge

Yield: 16 pieces | Prep Time: 5 minutes | Chill Time: 1 hour

It's hard to describe that texture when your teeth sink into a piece of fudge. It feels thick and dense, yet oddly light and dainty, perhaps because of the small size and the walnuts hidden inside. You don't need much to satisfy your sweet tooth craving, and the walnuts only add to the satisfying textural experience. This recipe is easy to make and you only have to wait an hour before digging in.

INGREDIENTS

1 (14-ounce) can sweetened condensed milk

1 (12-ounce) bag semisweet chocolate chips

1 teaspoon vanilla extract

1 cup walnuts, chopped

DIRECTIONS

1. Line an 8×8-inch baking dish with parchment paper.

2. In a microwave-safe bowl, combine the condensed milk, chocolate chips, and vanilla. Microwave on high for 1 minute. Stir and continue to microwave until the milk and chocolate come together.

3. Spread the mixture out on the lined baking sheet and place in the refrigerator. Allow to cool for 1 hour before cutting into squares.

Gummy Bears

Yield: 40 gummy bears | Prep Time: 15 minutes | Chill Time: 2 hours

You can buy gummy bears, but they are *so* fun to make. And the taste of a little homemade gummy bear is quite different than the pre-packaged kind. These bears are pastel in color and juicy as can be.

INGREDIENTS

1 cup berry fruit juice (or any fruit juice)

1 tablespoon lemon juice

3 (0.25-ounce) packets unflavored gelatin

¼ teaspoon sugar

Gummy bear molds (see Note)

DIRECTIONS

1. In a saucepan, bring the berry juice and lemon juice to a boil.

2. Add the gelatin and stir continuously for 3 minutes until dissolved.

3. Remove from the heat and stir in the sugar until dissolved.

4. Pour the mixture into gummy bear molds (see Note) and transfer to the refrigerator to set for at least 2 hours.

NOTE

Gummy bear molds are sold in craft stores and online.

Martha Washington Candies

Yield: 24 candies | Prep Time: 20 minutes | Chill Time: 1 hour

As the story goes, these candies came from Martha Washington's recipe collection. Not these very ones, as I have made a few changes myself, but this type of candy was created years ago and has become quite popular around Christmastime. Whether true or not, I enjoy picturing Martha and George passing these candies around as their guests dined.

INGREDIENTS

1½ cups pecans

1 cup sweetened flaked coconut

2 cups powdered sugar

4 tablespoons (½ stick / ¼ cup) unsalted butter, softened

1 (14-ounce) can sweetened condensed milk

2 cups melting chocolate wafers

DIRECTIONS

1. Line a baking sheet with parchment paper.

2. Place the pecans and coconut in a food processor and pulse until finely chopped.

3. Using a stand mixer fitted with the wire whip or a handheld mixer and a large bowl, cream together the sugar and butter. Add the milk and coconut-pecan mixture and mix until well combined.

4. Roll the mixture into small balls and place on the lined baking sheet.

5. Place in the refrigerator for at least 1 hour to firm up.

6. In a microwave-safe bowl, melt the chocolate on 50% power in 30-second increments, stirring in between, until melted.

7. Dip each ball into the chocolate coating using a fork, allowing the excess to drip back in the bowl when fishing out with a spoon.

8. Place on a sheet of parchment paper and continue dipping the candies until all are coated. Refrigerate until ready to eat.

Oreo Truffles

Yield: 24 truffles | Prep Time: 15 minutes | Chill Time: 1 hour

If there are Oreos out on the table, they tend to be gone before the last guest leaves. If there are Oreo truffles out, they might be gone before everyone arrives. Everything you know about an Oreo (white frosting sandwiched together with chocolate cookies) is flipped inside out to make a poppable, even richer chocolate snack.

INGREDIENTS

1 (14.3-ounce) package Oreos

1 (8-ounce) package cream cheese

1 cup mini chocolate chips

2 (12-ounce) packages white melting chocolate wafers

DIRECTIONS

1. Line a baking sheet with parchment paper.

2. In a food processor, pulse the Oreo cookies until completely crushed. Remove 1 cup and reserve for the topping.

3. Add the cream cheese and mini chocolate chips. Pulse to combine.

4. Form small balls of the mixture with your hands and place on the lined baking sheet.

5. Refrigerate for 1 hour. Remove.

6. In a microwave-safe bowl, microwave the white chocolate wafers on 50% power in 30-second increments until the chocolate has completely melted.

7. Top with the melted chocolate and the reserved crushed Oreos.

Peppermint Patties

Yield: 36 patties | Prep Time: 30 minutes | Chill Time: 2 hours

Patricia, also known as "Peppermint Patty," is part of the Snoopy crew. She is the tomboy in the group and is always running around with the boys. She reminds me of me when I was her age. I am not sure how her name relates to these little mint candies, but I'd guess it might have to do with the cool, fun taste inside the plain coating that surprises you every time.

INGREDIENTS

2½ cups powdered sugar

2 tablespoons unsalted butter, softened

2 teaspoons peppermint extract

2 tablespoons heavy whipping cream

Pink tinting gel (optional)

12 ounces melting chocolate wafers

Crushed peppermint candies (optional)

DIRECTIONS

1. Line two baking sheets with parchment paper.

2. In a stand mixer fitted with the paddle, beat the powdered sugar, butter, peppermint extract, and cream at medium speed until well combined. Increase the speed to high and beat until the mixture comes together and is light and creamy. If you want to tint the paste, add a small amount of the tinting gel with a toothpick or wooden skewer. Mix again until you achieve a color to your liking. The mixture should feel soft but firm enough to form into a log.

3. Scrape the candy paste onto a large piece of plastic wrap and form into a log 1½ inches in diameter. Wrap it well in the plastic wrap.

4. Chill the candy in the fridge until very firm, about 1 hour.

5. Using a sharp knife, slice the log into rounds about ¼ inch thick. Refrigerate for 1 hour.

6. Melt the chocolate on 50% power in 30-second increments, stirring in between each, until melted.

7. Remove the candy rounds from the refrigerator, a few at a time, and, using a fork, dip each candy round into the chocolate to coat, then remove, letting the excess chocolate drip off. Place on the second lined baking sheet. Sprinkle with crushed peppermint candies, if desired. Refrigerate for 5 minutes to allow the chocolate to harden before serving.

Rainbow Mint Bark

Yield: Serves 6 to 8 | Prep Time: 15 minutes | Chill Time: 30 minutes

I remember making bark from a torn-out magazine recipe when I was a kid. It was a Halloween recipe, where you loaded all your leftovers from trick-or-treating on top of a blank chocolate canvas. I thought it was such a cool idea—a good way to use up your candy, while also making something new. I make a bark of some sort for almost every party I throw. They vary in color and flavor, depending on the time of year. I made this rainbow variation for Easter and continue to make it throughout the summer.

INGREDIENTS

24 ounces white melting chocolate wafers

Red food coloring

1 cup mini nonpareil mint chips

1 cup mini marshmallows

DIRECTIONS

1. Line a baking sheet with parchment paper,

2. In a microwave-safe bowl, melt the white chocolate on 50% power in 30-second increments, stirring in between each, until melted. Place half the chocolate in a second bowl and tint it pink with red food coloring.

3. Pour the white chocolate on the lined baking sheet and pour the pink chocolate on top, swirling with a spoon or fork to marble.

4. Top with the mint chips and mini marshmallows.

5. Transfer to the fridge to cool and set for at least 30 minutes.

S'mores Bark

Yield: Serves 6 to 8 | Prep Time: 15 minutes | Chill Time: 1 hour

Most bachelorette parties include late nights at dark bars with bright signs. Mine, however, was on a vineyard and farm in Canada. We went "glamping," otherwise known as camping, but in a glamorous way. My girlfriends thought I was nuts when I made food consumption a priority at this party and created this amazingly simply but delicious camping bark. But it all got eaten!

INGREDIENTS

24 ounces melting chocolate wafers

6 full-size sheets graham crackers, crushed

2 cups mini marshmallows

1 cup store-bought caramel sauce

DIRECTIONS

1. Line a baking sheet with parchment paper.

2. In a microwave-safe bowl, melt the chocolate on 50% power in 30-second increments, stirring in between each, until melted. Pour the melted chocolate onto the lined baking sheet.

3. Sprinkle the crushed graham crackers and marshmallows on top.

4. Drizzle with the caramel sauce. Chill until the bark is hard enough to break apart, about 1 hour.

Sea Salted Caramels

Yield: 60 caramels | Prep Time: 15 minutes | Cook Time: 30 minutes

Caramel is super easy to make, and with a hint of sea salt, this delicious treat will not be made just once. Upon first bite, the salt opens up your taste buds and gets your tongue ready for the chewy, gooey caramel.

INGREDIENTS

2 cups light brown sugar, firmly packed

1 cup granulated sugar

1½ cups heavy whipping cream

16 tablespoons (2 sticks / 1 cup) unsalted butter

1 cup corn syrup

¼ cup bourbon

1 tablespoon vanilla extract

Pinch of coarse or flake sea salt

DIRECTIONS

1. Line a baking sheet with parchment paper.

2. Combine the sugars, cream, butter, corn syrup, and bourbon in a pot over medium heat.

3. Attach a candy thermometer. Bring to a simmer and cook until the thermometer registers 250°F.

4. Add the vanilla extract and salt. Cook for an additional 2 minutes.

5. Pour the caramel onto the lined baking sheet.

6. Transfer to the refrigerator to cool for at least two hours and set up. Remove the parchment paper from the baking sheet and set the caramels on a cutting board. Spray a sharp knife with cooking spray and cut into 1-inch squares. If wrapping, cut about sixty 4-inch squares out of plastic wrap. Place a caramel on the edge of a plastic square, roll it up, and twist the ends. Repeat for the remaining caramel pieces.

Salted Chocolate Peanut Clusters

Yield: 50 pieces | Prep Time: 15 minutes | Chill Time: 1 hour

These little clusters remind me of my grandmother. I think she bought hers at a local store, but they always seemed homemade. That is what I love about some of my childhood food memories. Just because something was store bought and/or semi-homemade doesn't mean it was any less special. The way you display or package it up, present it, and eat it, can be just as special as making it. This, however, is a very easy microwave candy, one made from scratch and with a lot of love.

INGREDIENTS

2 pounds white almond bark, broken into 1-inch pieces

1 (4-ounce) bar dark chocolate, broken into 1-inch pieces

12 ounces semisweet chocolate chips

4 cups salted and dry-roasted peanuts

Sea salt for garnish

DIRECTIONS

1. Line two baking sheets with aluminum foil or parchment paper.

2. In a large microwave-safe bowl, melt the white almond bark, dark chocolate, and semisweet chocolate chips on 50% power in 30-second increments, stirring in between each, until melted.

3. Stir in the peanuts. Scoop into clusters and place on the prepared baking sheets. Allow to cool at room temperature until set. Sprinkle with sea salt. Chill for 1 hour. Store in an airtight container in a cool place.

Truffles

Yield: 25 truffles | Prep Time: 40 minutes | Chill Time: 2 hours

If you're looking for a party favor, a holiday gift, or just a sweet treat to offer your guests after dinner, you've found it! Around the holidays, I gather my girlfriends to have a truffle-making, wine-drinking get-together. We then package them up and give them to the mailman, neighbors, dog walkers, and so on.

INGREDIENTS

1½ cups dark chocolate chips

½ cup heavy whipping cream

1 cup Nutella

2 cups milk chocolate melting chips

2 cups chopped candy-coated honey-roasted or butter toffee peanuts

DIRECTIONS

1. Put the dark chocolate chips in a large heatproof glass bowl.

2. Heat the heavy whipping cream in a medium saucepan over medium heat for 2 to 3 minutes. When hot, pour over the chocolate in the bowl and whisk to combine. Add the Nutella and continue to whisk until incorporated. Place in the refrigerator for 2 hours to set.

3. Once set, roll the mixture into 25 balls and set aside.

4. In a microwave-safe bowl, melt the milk chocolate on 50% power in 30-second increments, stirring in between each, until melted. Dip each truffle into the chocolate using a fork and roll them in a bowl with the chopped nuts.

Turtles

Yield: 25 turtles | Prep Time: 20 minutes | Chill Time: 15 minutes

Whoever saw these little treats and said they look like turtles was one smart cookie. Whenever I am making turtles, I just think of their namesake and remember that the four legs connected by a big mound of gooey caramel and a little head popping out is the way they should be.

INGREDIENTS

8 to 10 ounces pecan halves

25 caramels, unwrapped

¼ cup heavy whipping cream, plus extra if needed

½ teaspoon sea salt

⅓ cup dark chocolate chips

DIRECTIONS

1. Line two baking sheets with parchment paper.

2. For each turtle, place 5 pecans on the baking sheet, overlapping. They should look somewhat like a turtle with a head and four legs.

3. In a microwave-safe bowl, combine the caramels with half the cream. Microwave on high, stopping and stirring every 30 seconds, for 3 to 4 minutes until completely melted and smooth. Add the sea salt and stir to incorporate. If the mixture seems overly thick, add extra cream.

4. Spoon 1 tablespoon of the caramel over the pecans for each turtle.

5. In a microwave-safe bowl, melt the chocolate chips on high power in 30-second increments, stirring in between each, until melted. Spoon the melted chocolate over each cluster, covering as much or as little of the pecans as you like.

6. Allow the turtles to firm up at room temperature, or in the fridge or freezer for 15 minutes.

Cheesecake Jell-O Candies

Yield: 45 candies | Prep Time: 15 minutes | Chill Time: 1 hour

This is another one of my favorite candies to make, and the color possibilities are endless. In our house, Saint Nicholas comes early in the beginning of December to fill our shoes with sweet treats. It's an excuse for me to practice candy-making for Christmastime, and my husband doesn't complain when he wakes up to boots filled with goodies.

INGREDIENTS

1 (8-ounce) package cream cheese, at room temperature

1 cup powdered sugar

½ teaspoon lemon juice

2 tablespoons of two different Jell-O powders (color and flavor of your choice)

1 cup granulated sugar

DIRECTIONS

1. Line a baking sheet with parchment paper.

2. In a medium bowl, combine the cream cheese and powdered sugar. Add the lemon juice and stir.

3. Separate into two bowls and add 1 tablespoon of the Jell-O powder to each bowl.

4. Place the mixture into a piping bag and pipe little circles on the lined baking sheet.

5. Refrigerate for 1 hour.

6. Remove from the refrigerator and roll in the granulated sugar.

7. Store in an airtight container in the fridge for up to a week.

Cracker Candy

Yield: About 30 pieces | Prep Time: 15 minutes | Chill Time: 15 minutes

I love combining sweet and savory products, and using butter crackers to make a sweet treat is what gives this its name. I find that this works well as an appetizer, something that can sit out at any time of day.

INGREDIENTS

6 graham crackers

1 cup melting chocolate wafers

⅓ cup peanuts, crushed

1 cup butter crackers, crushed

1 teaspoon sea salt

DIRECTIONS

1. Line a baking sheet with parchment paper.

2. Break the graham crackers in half and lay them on the lined baking sheet.

3. In a microwave-safe bowl, melt the chocolate on high power in 30-second increments, stirring in between each, until melted. Pour the melted chocolate over the graham crackers on the baking sheet. Top with the peanuts and butter crackers.

4. Sprinkle with the sea salt. Set aside for about 15 minutes to set up, then break into pieces and serve.

Almond Brittle

Yield: Serves 8 to 10 | Prep Time: 15 minutes | Chill Time: 1 hour

A signature characteristic of parties at my house are the goodie bags. There is always a little something to-go for my guests, and this crunchy almond-coated treat is one that everyone tends to love. They are super easy to make and so cute wrapped up into individual baggies, tied with a pretty ribbon.

INGREDIENTS

8 tablespoons (1 stick / ½ cup) unsalted butter

½ cup sugar

1 tablespoon corn syrup

2 cups sliced almonds

DIRECTIONS

1. Line a 9 × 13-inch baking dish with parchment paper.

2. Combine the butter and sugar in a large saucepan over medium heat. Cook, stirring, until melted and combined.

3. Add the corn syrup and cook, stirring occasionally, until golden brown, about 5 minutes.

4. Reduce the heat to low, add the almond slices, and stir to combine.

5. Pour the mixture onto the lined baking sheet. The mixture will naturally spread out thinly, due to its consistency. Transfer to the refrigerator for 1 hour to cool and set up.

6. Break the brittle into pieces and package into individual servings, if desired.

Rock Candy

Yield: 4 candies | Prep Time: 45 minutes | Cook Time: 2 weeks

I remember learning about rocks as a kid and thinking that sugar turning into amazing crystal structures was truly like a science experiment. Rock candy is one of those treats that feels pretty magical because it is. This recipe is interactive, and while it does take time to grow your crystals, the wait is worth the beauty that occurs. It's a reminder that food is a science, and ingredients can create alchemy when they come together in the right way.

INGREDIENTS

Wooden skewers or string

2 cups water, plus extra for wetting the skewers

4 cups granulated sugar, plus extra for coating the skewers

1 teaspoon food coloring and/or 1 (0.125-ounce) flavoring oil (optional)

8-ounce glass jars

NOTE

If you have seen no change to your skewer or string after 24 hours, try boiling the sugar syrup again, dissolve another cup of sugar in it, then pour it back into the jar and insert the string or skewer again.

DIRECTIONS

1. Wet your wooden skewer, and roll it in granulated sugar. This base layer will give the sugar crystals something to "grab" when they start forming. Set the string or skewer aside to dry while you prepare your sugar syrup.

2. Bring the water to a boil in a medium saucepan. Begin adding the sugar, 1 cup at a time, stirring after each addition. You will notice that it takes longer for the sugar to dissolve. Bring the syrup to a boil and continue to stir until all the sugar has been added and it has dissolved. Remove the pan from the heat.

3. If you are using colors or flavorings, add them to the syrup at this point.

4. Allow the sugar syrup to cool for about 10 minutes, then pour it into the jars. Lower the sugared string or skewer until it hangs about 1 inch from the bottom.

5. Carefully place your jar in a cool place, away from harsh lights, where it can sit undisturbed. Cover the top loosely with plastic wrap.

6. Crystals will begin to form in the first 2 to 4 hours.

7. Allow the rock candy to grow until it is the size you want. Don't let it grow too large; otherwise, it might start growing into the sides of your jar! Once it has reached the size you want, remove it and allow it to dry for a few minutes, then enjoy or wrap in plastic wrap to save it for later.

Peanut Butter Fudge

Yield: 16 pieces | Prep Time: 15 minutes | Chill Time: 4 hours

There is never a time when peanut butter is not in our pantry. In fact, not just one jar but usually two twin-pack bulk-size ones just for backup. It would be a big-time fail if we were ever to run out, and if that were ever to happen, the look on my husband's face would reveal his broken heart. I don't know which one of us loves it more, but I have learned that peanut butter in everything makes it better.

INGREDIENTS

1 (12-ounce) bag peanut butter chips

1 (14-ounce) can condensed milk

2 tablespoons unsalted butter

2 teaspoons vanilla extract

1 (12-ounce) bag semisweet chocolate chips

DIRECTIONS

1. Line an 8×8-inch baking dish with parchment paper.

2. In a large microwave-safe bowl, melt the peanut butter chips, 1 cup of the condensed milk, 1 tablespoon of the butter, and 1 teaspoon of the vanilla on 50% power in 30-second increments, stirring in between each, until melted.

3. In a separate large microwave-safe bowl, melt the chocolate chips with the remaining condensed milk, 1 tablespoon butter, and 1 teaspoon vanilla on 50% power in 30-second increments, stirring in between each, until melted. Set aside.

4. Spread out the peanut butter fudge on the lined baking sheet, about ½ inch thick. Top with the chocolate fudge.

5. Using a fork or knife, swirl the two layers together to create a peanut-butter-and-chocolate-swirled fudge.

6. Transfer to the refrigerator for 4 hours to cool and set up. Cut into squares to serve.

Rainbow Puppy Chow

Yield: 12 to 16 servings | Prep Time: 15 minutes

Originally this type of dessert was called puppy chow because of its striking resemblance to dog food. We've made our version a little more special, and unlike dog food, this treat should be at every party. It's as if we threw confetti all over the coated cereal, and we sort of did. It only takes about 15 minutes to make, and the result is an instant party classic.

INGREDIENTS

1 cup white chocolate chips or white chocolate baking melts

1 (16-ounce) can premade vanilla frosting

1 (12-ounce) box Rice Chex cereal

3 tablespoons unsalted butter, melted

1 cup powdered sugar

1 cup sprinkles

DIRECTIONS

1. In a microwave-safe bowl, melt the white chocolate chips on 50% power in 30-second increments, stirring in between each, until melted. Set aside.

2. In a separate bowl, melt the frosting on 50% power in 30-second increments, stirring in between each, until melted. Set aside.

3. In a large bowl, toss the cereal with the melted butter.

4. Pour in the melted chocolate and vanilla frosting. Stir to coat all the cereal.

5. Add the powdered sugar and stir to coat.

6. Top with the sprinkles.

Gummy Champagne Hearts

Yield: 12 hearts | Prep Time: 15 minutes | Chill Time: 2 hours

My husband and I spent a few years dating long distance. When we were still in courting mode, I would do as many silly, yet sweet, things as I could think of during our limited time together. Making gummy champagne hearts to drink with champagne would fall into that category.

INGREDIENTS

1 cup champagne or prosecco

1 tablespoon lemon juice

3 (0.25-ounce) packets unflavored gelatin

¼ teaspoon granulated sugar

Edible gold glitter

DIRECTIONS

1. In a small saucepan, bring the champagne and lemon juice to a boil over medium heat.

2. Add the gelatin and stir continuously for 3 minutes until dissolved.

3. Remove from the heat and stir in the sugar until dissolved.

4. Pour the mixture into heart-shaped molds and transfer to the refrigerator to set for at least 2 hours.

5. Remove from the molds and brush with edible gold glitter (see Note).

NOTE

Edible glitter can be found online. Heart molds can be found at a craft store or online.

Ginger-Chocolate Hearts

Yield: 15 hearts | Prep Time: 15 minutes | Chill Time: 1 hour

This is another romantic way of making something super simple. The crystallized ginger sparkles and looks like the bubbles that come rushing to the top of the champagne glass—the perfect treat for a loved one.

INGREDIENTS

3 cups dark chocolate melting wafers

1 cup crushed hard ginger candy

Sea salt for garnish

DIRECTIONS

1. In a microwave-safe bowl, melt the chocolate on 50% power in 30-second increments, stirring in between each, until melted. Fold in ½ cup of the crushed ginger candy.

2. Place ½ teaspoon of the remaining ginger candy in each well of a heart mold (15 mini hearts in each mold; see Note) and pour the chocolate mixture over the top. Repeat until the mold is full.

3. Refrigerate for at least 1 hour.

4. To remove from the mold, place the mold upside-down and push the hearts out onto a plate or surface. Sprinkle with sea salt. Serve immediately or store in an airtight container for up to 2 weeks.

NOTE

Heart molds can be found at a craft store or online.

3

Cookies, Bites, and Bars

Cookies, and bites, and bars, oh my! All these little goodies are as good as they get, and you don't even have to turn your oven on. From cake batter balls to dipped sprinkle sandwiches, you'll find a sweet treat in here for every occasion.

Funfetti Cake Batter Bites

Yield: 30 truffles | Prep Time: 30 minutes | Chill Time: 30 minutes

For our wedding, I wanted a vanilla cake with vanilla frosting. The baker made one for us to try, and my feedback was, "Can it be more like a box mix?" Despite understanding a sophisticated taste, there are some things that don't need any upgrade, and a vanilla cake made out of a boxed mix is one of them. These little batter balls bring that cake mix essence into a one-bite form.

INGREDIENTS

8 tablespoons (1 stick / ½ cup) unsalted butter, softened

1½ cups Funfetti cake mix

½ cup sugar

½ cup all-purpose flour

2 teaspoons vanilla extract or vanilla bean paste

¼ cup rainbow nonpareils

16 ounces white chocolate melting wafers or CandyQuik

Rainbow nonpareils, coconut, or chopped nuts (optional)

DIRECTIONS

1. Line a baking sheet with parchment paper.

2. In the bowl of a food processor, combine the butter, cake mix, sugar, flour, and vanilla. Process until it forms a firm dough. Transfer to a bowl.

3. Mix the nonpareils into the dough.

4. Roll the dough into 1-inch balls and place on the lined baking sheet.

5. Freeze the dough balls for 10 minutes.

6. In a microwave-safe bowl, melt the white chocolate on 50% power in 30-second increments, stirring in between each, until melted. Dip the cake balls into the melted chocolate, remove with a fork, and place back on the lined baking sheet.

7. Sprinkle the tops with the nonpareils, coconut, or chopped nuts.

8. Let the cake truffles harden at room temperature or in the fridge for 20 minutes before serving.

Peanut Butter Cheesecake Bites

Yield: 24 bites | Prep Time: 15 minutes | Chill Time: 1 hour

These taste like homemade peanut butter cups! They're one of my favorite treats to make and serve on any occasion.

INGREDIENTS

8 ounces cream cheese, at room temperature

1 cup peanut butter cups, coarsely chopped

¼ cup creamy peanut butter

¼ cup vanilla ice cream

3 tablespoons mini chocolate chips

DIRECTIONS

1. Combine all of the ingredients in the bowl of a stand mixer fitted with the paddle and beat for 5 minutes on medium speed. Alternatively, mix all the ingredients in a large bowl using a handheld mixer on high for 5 minutes.

2. Spoon the mixture into a peanut butter cup silicone mold (see Note) and top with chocolate chips. Refrigerate for an hour to cool and firm.

3. Once chilled, pop out the mini cups and place in mini cupcake liners to serve.

NOTE

Peanut butter cup molds can be purchased at a craft store or online.

Coconut Praline Bites

Yield: 40 cookies | Prep Time: 20 minutes | Chill Time: 1 to 2 hours

I made these for the first time on a cold winter day. They remind me of the slick, shiny ice rink that would form over our backyard when we hosed it down in the freezing cold to form a place to play hockey. It's an adult treat for a *Frozen* party and a gooey little bite between sips of hot cocoa.

INGREDIENTS

2½ cups coarsely chopped pecans

2 cups sweetened shredded coconut

5 ounces dried cherries

2½ cups sugar

½ cup evaporated milk

½ cup corn syrup

8 tablespoons (1 stick / ½ cup) unsalted butter

1 teaspoon vanilla extract

Sanding sugar, for serving

DIRECTIONS

1. Line an 8 × 8-inch baking dish with aluminum foil or parchment paper.

2. In a large bowl, combine the pecans, coconut, and cherries and stir to combine.

3. In a medium saucepan, cook the sugar, evaporated milk, corn syrup, and butter over medium-high heat, stirring until it boils. Let it boil, undisturbed, for 3 minutes.

4. Remove from the heat and add to the bowl with the pecans, coconut, and cherries. Stir for 3 minutes until cooled and thickened.

5. Press the mixture into the baking dish.

6. Transfer to the refrigerator to harden for at least 1 to 2 hours. Remove the mixture from the baking dish, set on a cutting board, and cut into 1-inch squares. Serve, sprinkled with sanding sugar.

Cookie Dough Brownie Bites

Yield: 48 bites | Prep Time: 45 minutes | Chill Time: 30 minutes

Eating the cookie dough before it went in the oven was always my favorite part about baking. These brownie bites, stuffed with dough, are a more sanctioned way to do just that. With no eggs, it is perfectly safe to eat unbaked!

INGREDIENTS

8 tablespoons (1 stick) unsalted butter, softened

½ cup light brown sugar, firmly packed

3 ounces cream cheese

½ cup creamy peanut butter

¼ cup granulated sugar

2 teaspoons vanilla extract

¼ teaspoon baking soda

¼ teaspoon salt

1¼ cups all-purpose flour

1 (18.3-ounce) box brownie mix

½ (16-ounce) container chocolate frosting

¾ cup mini chocolate chips

3 cups milk or semisweet chocolate chips

1 teaspoon coconut oil

DIRECTIONS

1. Beat together the butter and brown sugar. Beat in the cream cheese, peanut butter, and granulated sugar. Add the vanilla, baking soda, salt, and flour and blend well. Stir in the mini chocolate chips.

2. Roll the cookie dough into 48 small balls and set aside.

3. Prepare the brownie mix, according to package directions. Cool completely and crumble into a bowl. Add the frosting and mix until combined.

4. Roll each cookie dough ball in the brownie mixture and form into a ball. Place in the fridge on a parchment paper–lined baking sheet while preparing the coating.

5. Combine the milk chocolate chips with the coconut oil in a microwave-safe bowl. Heat on high for 30 seconds, stir, and continue to microwave in 15-second increments until melted and smooth.

6. Dip each ball into the chocolate coating using a toothpick. Place back on the baking sheet and sprinkle with mini chocolate chips.

7. Refrigerate for 5 to 10 minutes before serving.

Energy Bites

Yield: 12 bites | Prep Time: 10 minutes | Chill Time: 1 hour

This is another one of my "glamping" food items, perfect for hiking, beach sitting, pitching a tent (not that I know how to do that), and riding horses. Fifteen happy ladies spent four days in Canada in tents nicer than my home with produce from my garden and wine from the vineyards we visited. We ate our fair share of these little bites of energy to keep us going from activity to activity, and they were the perfect snack for the plane ride home.

INGREDIENTS

¼ cup graham cracker crumbs

2 tablespoons unsalted butter, melted

¼ cup old-fashioned oats

¼ cup raisins

½ cup creamy peanut butter

DIRECTIONS

1. Line a baking sheet with parchment paper.

2. In a medium bowl, combine the graham cracker crumbs, butter, oats, raisins, and peanut butter.

3. Using your hands, roll the dough into small balls, about 1 inch in diameter, and place on the lined baking sheet.

4. Refrigerate for 1 hour before serving.

Butterscotch Haystacks

Yield: 100 haystacks | Prep Time: 30 minutes | Cook Time: 10 minutes

I hosted a western-themed party one night, as my husband and I both wish we had reasons to wear our cowboy boots daily, and these little haystacks fit in well with the bandanas and horse-themed decorations.

INGREDIENTS

1 (11-ounce) package butterscotch chips

1 (10-ounce) package peanut butter chips

1 (11-ounce) package white chocolate chips

½ cup creamy peanut butter

12 ounces salted cocktail peanuts or sea salt–caramel peanuts

12 ounces dry canned chow mein noodles

DIRECTIONS

1. Line three baking sheets with parchment paper.

2. Combine the butterscotch chips, peanut butter chips, white chocolate chips, and peanut butter in a large saucepan. Place over low heat and cook, stirring, until the mixture is melted and smooth, about 10 minutes.

3. Remove from the heat and fold in the peanuts and chow mein noodles.

4. Using a small spring-loaded scoop, drop clumps of the mixture onto the baking sheet.

5. Set aside at room temperature for 20 to 30 minutes until firm before serving.

Nutella Bars

Yield: 12 to 16 bars | Prep Time: 15 minutes | Chill Time: 3 hours

Keep these tucked away in the freezer, and when you come home late at night and find them hidden in the back, it's as if you've struck snacking gold—sticky, chocolaty, nutty gold.

INGREDIENTS

2 cups sugar

½ cup whole milk

8 tablespoons (1 stick / ½ cup) unsalted butter

¼ cup unsweetened cocoa powder

3 cups quick-cooking oatmeal

¼ cup creamy peanut butter

¼ cup Nutella

1 teaspoon vanilla extract

⅛ teaspoon kosher salt

DIRECTIONS

1. Line a 9 × 13-inch baking dish with parchment paper.

2. In a small saucepan, combine the sugar, milk, butter, and cocoa powder over medium heat and stir to combine. Bring to a boil and boil, undisturbed, for 1 minute.

3. Remove the pan from the heat and stir in the oatmeal, peanut butter, Nutella, vanilla, and salt until well mixed.

4. Press the batter onto the lined baking sheet and place in the refrigerator. Chill for 3 hours to set before slicing into bars.

Pumpkin Cheesecake Balls

Yield: 16 balls | Prep Time: 20 minutes | Chill Time: 1 hour 30 minutes

Pumpkin doesn't have to be just for pies, nor does it need to be limited to just the fall months. These light cheesecake balls are just as delightful in the summertime.

INGREDIENTS

18 ounces white chocolate melting wafers

¾ cup vanilla cookie crumbs or graham cracker crumbs

½ cup pure pumpkin puree

6 ounces cream cheese, at room temperature

¼ cup powdered sugar

1 teaspoon pumpkin pie spice

½ cup milk

Milk chocolate chips, melted (optional)

DIRECTIONS

1. Line a baking sheet with parchment paper.

2. In a microwave-safe bowl, melt the white chocolate on 50% power in 30-second increments, stirring in between each, until melted.

3. Place the cookie crumbs, pumpkin, cream cheese, powdered sugar, and pumpkin pie spice into the bowl of a stand mixer fitted with the paddle and mix on medium speed, scraping down the sides of the bowl, for 2 minutes. Alternatively, you can use a hand mixer and mix on high for 2 minutes, stopping occasionally to scrape down the sides of the bowl.

4. Add ½ cup of the melted chocolate and mix for 2 minutes. Cover the bowl with plastic wrap, transfer to the refrigerator, and chill for at least 30 minutes. While the mixture chills, remove the melted chocolate from the heat.

5. To form, use a small scoop or round spoon and form the mixture into 16 balls. Place them on the lined baking sheet. Using your fingertips, smooth out any rough edges.

6. Place in the freezer for 1 hour.

7. Reheat the chocolate in the microwave on high for 1 minute. Using a fork or an offset spatula, lower each ball into the melted chocolate and turn to coat. Remove from the bowl, letting the excess chocolate drip back into the bowl, and transfer the coated ball to the lined baking sheet. Repeat to make 16 balls.

8. Keep in the freezer until hardened. Drizzle with melted milk chocolate, if desired. Refreeze and serve.

Snickerdoodle Balls

Yield: 20 balls | Prep Time: 15 minutes | Chill Time: 1 hour

My husband and I have a "Labradoodle," also known as a doodle, and her name is Paisley. My in-laws have her sister, whose name is Sophie, but we all call her Snickerdoodle. My sister-in-law and her husband adopted her brother, Hunter, who we call a string bean. This sounds silly, and it is, but whenever I hear the word *snickerdoodle*, I think of our three sweet little furry pups and can't help but smile. You may feel the same way once you try these little balls of joy. Plus, they are healthy and full of whole, nutritious ingredients.

INGREDIENTS

1 cup whole raw cashews

½ cup raw almonds

¼ cup flaked sweetened coconut

2 teaspoons ground cinnamon

½ teaspoon ground nutmeg

¼ teaspoon sea salt

10 ounces Medjool dates, pitted

¼ teaspoon coconut extract

DIRECTIONS

1. Line a baking sheet with parchment paper.

2. Using a food processor fitted with the "S" blade, process the cashews, almonds, flaked coconut, cinnamon, nutmeg, and salt until finely ground.

3. Add the dates and coconut extract and process until the dough becomes very sticky.

4. Using a small spring-loaded scoop or a tablespoon, scoop the mixture and roll it in your hands to form a smooth ball; repeat to make 20 balls.

5. Place the balls on the lined baking sheet and transfer to the fridge or freezer for 1 hour.

6. Store the snack bites in the fridge for up to 2 weeks.

Cookie Sandwiches

Yield: 12 cookie sandwiches | Prep Time: 5 minutes | Assemble Time: 10 minutes

If you are in need of a very last-minute dessert, look no further than these bite-size cookies filled with vanilla frosting and rolled in sprinkles. Customize these your way with different types of cookies, frostings, and candies to coat them.

INGREDIENTS

1 (16-ounce) can vanilla frosting

24 mini sugar cookies

2 cups mini chocolate candies or sprinkles

DIRECTIONS

1. Place the vanilla frosting in a piping bag fitted with a plain tip or in a zip-top plastic bag with a cut corner.

2. Pipe the frosting onto one cookie and sandwich with another cookie.

3. Roll the edges of the cookie sandwiches in the candies or sprinkles. Arrange on a plate and serve.

Dipped Cookies

Yield: 24 cookies | Prep Time: 15 minutes | Chill Time: 30 minutes

By now you may think that our house is covered in sprinkles and confetti, and you wouldn't be wrong. Those two items alone can take any premade, store-bought item and make it photo-worthy. This is an adorable example.

INGREDIENTS

12 ounces white chocolate, melted

24 mini chocolate chip cookies

1 cup sprinkles

DIRECTIONS

1. Line a baking sheet with parchment paper.

2. In a microwave-safe bowl, melt the white chocolate on 50% power in 30-second increments, stirring in between each, until melted. Dip a cookie halfway into the white chocolate and transfer to the lined baking sheet.

3. Decorate with sprinkles and place in the refrigerator to set for about 30 minutes.

VARIATIONS

Instead of a white chocolate dip, try dark chocolate, butterscotch, or peanut butter chips!

Chocolate Oatmeal Cookies

Yield: Makes 24 cookies | Prep Time: 10 minutes | Cook Time: 1 hour

I love eating cookies year-round, but when the temperature spikes above 80°F, the last thing I want to do is turn on the oven. These no-bake cookies satisfy my cookie cravings without turning my kitchen into a sauna! Plus, the coconut makes these cookies even sweeter than regular chocolate oatmeal cookies.

INGREDIENTS

2 cups old-fashioned oats

⅔ cup creamy peanut butter

1 cup sweetened flaked coconut

¼ cup cocoa powder

¼ teaspoon instant espresso powder

1 teaspoon vanilla extract

Pinch of salt

2 cups sugar

½ cup whole milk

4 tablespoons (½ stick/ ¼ cup) unsalted butter

DIRECTIONS

1. In a medium bowl, combine the oats, peanut butter, coconut, cocoa powder, espresso powder, vanilla, and salt. Stir until evenly mixed.

2. Line two baking sheets with wax paper and set aside.

3. In a large microwave-safe glass bowl, combine the sugar, milk, and butter. Microwave for 3 to 4 minutes on high until the mixture is thick and bubbly. Be careful removing from the microwave as the dish will be hot and the mixture extremely molten.

4. Pour the mixture over the oats. Mix together quickly and then, using a spoon, scoop onto the baking sheets. Allow to sit for 1 hour until the cookies are cooled and set.

5. Serve or store in an airtight container in a cool place, up to 3 days.

Loaded Marshmallow Cereal Treats

Yield: Serves 6 to 8 | Prep Time: 15 minutes | Chill Time: 30 minutes

I used to think that eating a cereal treat was the same as eating cereal because I was convinced that the marshmallows holding it all together were just another form of milk. I thought this was the best breakfast in the world. When you fold in and top it with sprinkles, I suppose I should have realized it was not the healthiest of breakfasts, but it remains one of the tastiest treats.

INGREDIENTS

8 tablespoons (1 stick / ½ cup) unsalted butter

1 (10-ounce) bag mini marshmallows

1 (12-ounce) box Kix cereal

Sprinkles

DIRECTIONS

1. Line a 9-inch cake pan with parchment paper.

2. Melt the butter in a large pot over medium heat. Add three-quarters of the marshmallows and stir.

3. Turn the heat to low and add the cereal and three-quarters of the sprinkles. Stir to combine.

4. Once combined, pour the mixture into the lined cake pan.

5. Top with the remaining marshmallows and sprinkles and let cool to room temperature. Chill for 30 minutes.

6. Slice into squares to serve.

VARIATION

Switch out the Kix for your favorite cereal.

Oreo No-Bake Cheesecake Bars

Yield: 16 bites | Prep Time: 15 minutes | Chill Time: 1 hour

Cookies-and-cream is my favorite flavor of ice cream, although it has always been a tough draw between that and vanilla with sprinkles. I don't eat ice cream as often as I should, and when I make these little bars, I am reminded of that flavor from the summers as a kid when we rode our bikes to a little shop, and I'd emerge triumphantly with a heaping scoop of my favorite treat.

INGREDIENTS

1 (8-ounce) package cream cheese

1 gallon cookies-and-cream ice cream

10 Oreo cookies

DIRECTIONS

1. In the bowl of a stand mixer fitted with the paddle, combine the cream cheese and ice cream. Beat on high for 5 minutes.

2. Pour the mixture into a 9-inch cake pan and freeze for 1 hour.

3. Remove from the freezer and top with crushed Oreos. Dip your knife in hot water before cutting into bars. Serve.

Peanut Butter Bars

Yield: 12 to 16 bars | Prep Time: 15 minutes | Chill Time: 4 hours

If my husband had his way, he would eat chocolate ice cream with peanut butter and M&Ms for dessert every night, so thank goodness my experimentations, like these bars, have added a little variety to our peanut butter consumption.

INGREDIENTS

8 tablespoons (1 stick / ½ cup) unsalted butter, melted

1 cup graham cracker crumbs

1 cup powdered sugar

1 cup creamy peanut butter

½ cup semisweet chocolate chips

½ cup peanut butter chips, plus extra for garnish

White chocolate chips for garnish

DIRECTIONS

1. Line an 8 × 8-inch square pan with aluminum foil.

2. In a medium bowl, combine the melted butter, graham cracker crumbs, and powdered sugar. Add the peanut butter and stir to combine. Spread the mixture into the prepared baking pan.

3. In a small microwaveable bowl, melt the semisweet chocolate chips with ½ cup of the peanut butter chips on 50% power in 30-second increments, stirring in between each, until melted.

4. Pour the melted chocolate on top of the peanut butter bars and refrigerate for at least 4 hours or until the bars are set.

5. Remove from the refrigerator, cut into squares, and top with peanut butter chips and white chocolate chips.

Bourbon Pecan Bars

Yield: Makes ten to twelve 3-inch bars | Prep Time: 25 minutes | Chill Time: 1 hour

Last year when I cooked at the Kentucky Derby, I had my first slice of Derby Pie and tasted true trail bourbon. I wanted to bring a few of these memories back home to share with friends and family, and these bars embody my food experience: slightly salty and super sweet, with a shot of tough love.

INGREDIENTS

1 (13.5-ounce) package graham cracker crust box mix

¼ cup cornstarch

1 cup light brown sugar, firmly packed

1 cup water

½ cup bourbon

2 large egg yolks

1 teaspoon kosher salt

3 tablespoons unsalted butter

1 teaspoon vanilla extract

2 cups chopped pecans

DIRECTIONS

1. Prepare the graham cracker crust according to the box directions.

2. In a medium saucepan, combine the cornstarch, brown sugar, water, bourbon, and egg yolks.

3. Simmer over medium heat, stirring constantly, until melted and thickened. Boil for 1 minute, continuing to stir constantly. Add the salt.

4. Remove from the heat and stir in the butter, vanilla, and pecans.

5. Pour the filling into the prepared graham cracker crust and refrigerate for 1 hour.

6. To serve, cut into thin 3-inch bars.

Lemon Bars

Yield: Makes ten to twelve 3-inch bars | Prep Time: 15 minutes | Chill Time: 2 hours

Lemon bars have been around as long as lemonade stands, and I am sure you have tried one or two. What I love about this classic recipe is that you don't need to turn the oven on during a summer heat wave, and served chilled, they will taste like lemonade from the stand down the street.

INGREDIENTS

1 (13.5-ounce) package graham cracker crust box mix

1¼ cups granulated sugar

4 large eggs

1 cup lemon juice

8 tablespoons (1 stick / ½ cup) unsalted butter, melted

½ cup powdered sugar

Lemon slices

DIRECTIONS

1. Prepare the graham cracker crust according to the box directions.

2. In a medium microwave-safe bowl, combine the granulated sugar and eggs. Pour in the lemon juice and melted butter and stir to combine.

3. Microwave on high for about 6 minutes, checking every minute and stirring with a spoon until the lemon curd coats the back of the spoon.

4. Pour the curd into the prepared graham cracker crust and freeze for 2 hours.

5. Remove from the freezer, top with the powdered sugar and lemon slices. Cut into 3-inch bars and serve.

4

Fruit and Frozen Desserts

Fruit and frozen treats make for refreshing, light, and vibrantly bright desserts. We all know those bold colors that stare us in the face when we enter the fruit section of a grocery store. The naturally brilliant hues can't be replaced in any other way, and I love incorporating berries on a hot summer day or citrus to brighten a cold snowy night. The frozen desserts in this chapter range in shape and size, and you'll find something for everyone. Whether it be a no-churn ice cream or a grasshopper pie, the options are vast, simple, and not as sticky as you may think!

Banana Split

Yield: 4 banana splits | Prep Time: 10 minutes | Chill Time: n/a

Banana splits remind me of dating in the '50s, at least the version I have seen on TV and in movies like *Grease* with high school students sharing a spoon or straw and enjoying a sweet treat. Life back then sounds a lot simpler than the dating that goes on today, and when I make this dessert for two, I feel like those kids, too.

INGREDIENTS

1 cup graham cracker crumbs

8 tablespoons (1 stick / ½ cup) unsalted butter, melted

3 large bananas, peeled and sliced lengthwise

1 (20-ounce) can crushed pineapple, drained

3 cups fresh strawberries (about 1 pound), hulled and sliced ¼ inch thick

1 (12-ounce) container frozen whipped topping, thawed

DIRECTIONS

1. In a medium bowl, combine the graham cracker crumbs with the melted butter. Press ¼ cup of the mixture on the bottom of each of four small rectangular glass dishes. They should be about 6 to 8 inches long.

2. Top each with a banana half and ¼ cup of the drained pineapple. Add an even layer of the sliced strawberries.

3. Spread a layer of whipped topping on top. Slice the remaining banana halves into ½-inch chunks. Garnish with additional graham crackers, bananas, pineapple, and strawberry. Serve immediately.

Fruit Kabobs with Dips

Yield: 6 kabobs with 2 dips | Prep Time: 15 minutes | Cook Time: 2 minutes

Naughty or nice? You have two dipping choices here—a rich, decadent chocolate coating with agave or Greek yogurt sweetened with honey. Choose your favorite fruits and set outside for everyone to enjoy.

INGREDIENTS

1 (5.3-ounce) container Greek yogurt

¼ cup honey

12 ounces melting chocolate wafers

¼ cup agave syrup

Assorted fruits, cut into kabob-size pieces

DIRECTIONS

1. Combine the yogurt and honey and set aside.

2. In a microwave-safe bowl, melt the chocolate on 50% power in 30-second increments, stirring in between each, until melted. Add the agave and mix to combine. Set aside.

3. Skewer the assorted fruits on wooden skewers. Serve alongside the two dips.

Mini Fruit Tarts

Yield: 4 mini tarts | Prep Time: 15 minutes | Chill Time: 2 hours

Fit for the fanciest garden party but made with store-bought graham cracker crusts and just a few ingredients, these are ideal for bridal showers, birthday parties, and summer soirees.

INGREDIENTS

¾ cup cold heavy whipping cream

1 cup mascarpone cheese

1 tablespoon sugar

1 teaspoon vanilla extract

4 store-bought mini graham cracker crusts

Mixed fresh berries and parsley for garnish

DIRECTIONS

1. In the bowl of a stand mixer fitted with the wire whip, whip the heavy whipping cream until soft peaks form. Alternatively, use a large bowl and a handheld mixer or whisk. Set the whipped cream aside.

2. In a separate large bowl, combine the mascarpone cheese, sugar, and vanilla and whisk until smooth.

3. Fold the whipped cream into the mascarpone mixture by hand.

4. Divide the filling equally among the mini graham crusts.

5. Refrigerate the tarts for 2 hours.

6. Garnish the tarts with the fresh berries and parsley to serve.

Raspberry-Lemon Meltaways

Yield: Serves 16 | Prep Time: 15 minutes | Chill Time: Overnight

They may look like they are melting away, thus the name, but believe me when I say they will be gobbled up before they do. A perfectly cut square brownie sure is beautiful, but a dessert that is meant to slip and slide delivers on something else: fun!

INGREDIENTS

20 lemon Oreo cookies, plus extra for garnish

12 tablespoons (1½ stick / ¾ cup) unsalted butter, softened

2½ cups powdered sugar

½ cup fresh raspberries

2 tablespoons seedless raspberry jelly

2 tablespoons finely grated lemon zest

DIRECTIONS

1. In a food processor, grind the cookies into crumbs. Add the butter and pulse until the mixture resembles wet sand. Press into a 7 × 11-inch baking pan, using your fingertips or the bottom of a measuring cup to make a solid, flat surface.

2. In the same food processor bowl (no need to wash), process the powdered sugar, raspberries, raspberry jelly, and lemon zest until smooth. Spread evenly over the crust.

3. Cover lightly with plastic wrap and refrigerate overnight. Grind a few extra Oreos in the food processor to make crumbs. Sprinkle on top before cutting into squares to serve.

Stuffed Strawberries

Yield: 20 to 24 stuffed strawberries │ Prep Time: 15 minutes │ Chill Time: n/a

One summer, I taught the kids next door how to make these. It was fun watching them remove the center of the strawberry, making a little hollow hat or cone to fill with delicious creamy centers. It's a great interactive dessert and perfect for picnics and outdoor barbecues.

INGREDIENTS

20 to 24 large fresh strawberries

4 ounces cream cheese, at room temperature

¼ cup powdered sugar

¼ teaspoon vanilla extract

½ cup mini chocolate chips

DIRECTIONS

1. Hull the strawberries and hollow out the center using a paring knife or small melon baller. Set on paper towels, cut-side down, while you prepare the filling.

2. Using an electric mixer, whip the cream cheese, powdered sugar, and vanilla until smooth. Spoon into a piping bag with a small plain tip or into a zip-top plastic bag with one corner cut off. Pipe the filling into each berry, leaving a mound on top.

3. Sprinkle with mini chocolate chips. Store in plastic containers in the fridge for up to 2 days or serve immediately.

Healthy Fruit Pizza

Yield: 1 pizza pie; serves 6 to 8 | Prep Time: 15 minutes | Chill Time: 2 hours

I love grilling pizza, and on Saturdays in the summer when that is the star of date night, I often make this fruit pizza to accompany the theme. It is a light and refreshing way to follow up the rich sausage-and-tomato-topped charred dough.

INGREDIENTS

1½ cups cornflakes

1 cup pecans

⅓ cup corn syrup

¼ cup powdered sugar

8 ounces cream cheese, at room temperature

4 ounces Greek yogurt

1 tablespoon orange juice

1 tablespoon granulated sugar, plus more if needed

Assorted fruit for topping

DIRECTIONS

1. In a food processor, combine the cornflakes, pecans, corn syrup, and powdered sugar. Pulse until combined and the cornflakes and pecans are finely chopped.

2. Press the mixture into the bottom of a 9-inch springform pan or pie plate to form a crust.

3. In the bowl of a stand mixer fitted with the paddle, beat the cream cheese, yogurt, orange juice, and granulated sugar until well combined. Taste and add more sugar if you would like.

4. Evenly spread the cream cheese–yogurt mixture over the crust.

5. Top with assorted fruits and refrigerate for at least 2 hours. Release from the springform pan or pie plate and slice into wedges to serve.

No-Bake Lemon Berry Bars

Yield: 1 pie; makes ten to twelve 3-inch bars | Prep Time: 15 minutes | Chill Time: 4 hours

Despite how easy these are to make, they look like they came from a quaint French patisserie like the one that I frequented while living in France. I will never forget those bright little tarts staring at me as I strolled by the little window fronts in Avignon. Years later, these picture-perfect little lemon berry bars are my go-to for hosting ladies' lunches or showers.

INGREDIENTS

1 (3.4-ounce) package instant lemon pudding mix

1 (13.5-ounce) package graham cracker crust box mix

1 (8-ounce) container frozen whipped topping, thawed

Assorted fresh berries

DIRECTIONS

1. Make the pudding according to the package directions.

2. Prepare the graham cracker crust in a 9 × 9-inch baking dish, according to the box directions.

3. Pour the lemon pudding filling into the graham cracker crust and refrigerate for 4 hours.

4. Remove from the fridge and spoon the whipped topping over the set pudding layer.

5. If you'd like the whipped topping to resemble a traditional meringue topping, torch the top lightly. Using a kitchen blowtorch with a medium flame, pass over the topping on the bars, just barely above the surface, working in a circular pattern, until the surface turns a light golden brown.

6. Arrange the berries on top and cut into 3-inch bars. Serve immediately.

NOTE

Pick the freshest berries in season for the tastiest dessert.

Crème Brûlée

Yield: Six 4-ounce crèmes | Prep Time: 15 minutes | Chill Time: 3 hours or overnight

Crème brûlée is one of those food items that you see on restaurant menus but rarely indulge in at home. If you have a blowtorch, it's a dramatic way to end the evening!

INGREDIENTS

1 cup heavy whipping cream

½ cup whole milk

½ cup granulated sugar

1 vanilla bean, cut in half and seeds scraped and reserved

4 large egg yolks

2 tablespoons cornstarch

6 tablespoons superfine sugar

Sliced strawberries for garnish

DIRECTIONS

1. In a medium nonstick saucepan, stir together the cream, milk, granulated sugar, and vanilla bean seeds and pod. Heat gently over medium-low heat until you see steam and small bubbles form around the edges of the pot; do not boil.

2. While the cream mixture heats, put the egg yolks in a large bowl and whisk in the cornstarch to make a smooth paste. When the cream mixture is heated, pour it through a fine-mesh sieve into a measuring cup and set aside to cool for 2 minutes. Very gradually add the cream mixture to the yolk mixture, whisking constantly.

3. Return to the pan and cook over medium heat, stirring constantly with a rubber scraper, and scraping the bottom and sides so it does not scorch. Cook and stir for about 5 minutes or until the mixture has thickened enough to coat the scraper.

4. Remove the pan from the heat and again pour it through the fine-mesh sieve to remove any lumps. Discard the vanilla bean pod.

5. Gently pour the custard into six shallow 4-inch ramekins set on a baking sheet. Cool to room temperature, then lightly cover with plastic wrap and chill for 3 hours or overnight.

6. When ready to serve, remove the plastic wrap and top each custard with 1 tablespoon of the superfine sugar, applying it in an even layer thick enough to completely cover the surface. Using a kitchen blowtorch with a medium flame, pass over each custard just barely above the sugar surface, working in a circular pattern, until the sugar melts and becomes a dark golden brown. Serve, garnished with strawberries.

Blueberry Crunch Cake

Yield: 1 cake; serves 8 to 10 | Prep Time: 15 minutes | Chill Time: 4 hours or overnight

This is a perfect example of the beauty of ingredients coming together to create a dish that's more than the sum of its parts. This is one of my favorites for morning and daytime treats, especially paired with a mimosa!

INGREDIENTS

25 graham crackers, crushed, plus extra for garnish

8 tablespoons (1 stick / ½ cup) unsalted butter, melted

½ cup sugar

1 (8-ounce) package cream cheese, at room temperature

¼ cup lemon juice

1 (8-ounce) container frozen whipped topping, thawed

1 cup fresh blueberries, plus extra for garnish

DIRECTIONS

1. In a medium bowl, mix the graham crackers with the melted butter and sugar, using a fork.

2. Press the mixture into the bottom of a 9-inch round cake pan to form a crust.

3. In the bowl of a stand mixer fitted with the paddle, combine the cream cheese, lemon juice, whipped topping, and blueberries.

4. Spread the cream cheese mixture on top of the crust and refrigerate the cake for 4 hours or overnight.

5. Top with the remaining crushed graham crackers and blueberries, slice, and serve.

Frozen Fruit Cups

Yield: 12 fruit cups | Prep Time: 15 minutes | Chill Time: 2 hours

Trick those kiddos! I made these for the neighbor boys, and they thought they were eating candy. "Health stealth foods" is what I call them. Make these ahead of time and pull them out of the freezer when everyone behaves, clears their plate, and says, "Please!"

INGREDIENTS

1 (8-ounce) container frozen whipped topping, thawed

2 cups frozen raspberries

1 cup vanilla ice cream

DIRECTIONS

1. Combine the whipped topping, raspberries, and ice cream in a blender and blend on medium until smooth.

2. Pour into mini cupcake tins, lined with paper liners, and place in the freezer for 2 hours. Remove from the freezer and serve.

Mini Lemon Meringue Pies

Yield: 12 mini pies | Prep Time: 25 minutes | Chill Time: Overnight

Lemon curd and meringue are easier to make than I imagined when going into culinary school. I was always intimidated by pastries. As a young culinary student, there seemed to be a gazillion reasons why pastries flop, and until I realized that there are simpler techniques and shortcuts, I thought that something like this would be too challenging to try. I've taken what I learned back then and simplified it for my own ease and yours.

INGREDIENTS

1 cup sugar

3 large eggs

Finely grated lemon zest

1 cup lemon juice

8 tablespoons (1 stick / ½ cup) unsalted butter, melted

12 store-bought mini graham cracker crusts

1 (3.5-ounce) package lemon pudding mix

1 (8-ounce) container frozen whipped topping, thawed

Lemons for garnish

Granulated suger

DIRECTIONS

1. In a large microwave-safe bowl, whisk together the sugar and eggs until smooth and well combined. Whisk in the lemon zest, lemon juice, and butter.

2. Cook in the microwave on full power in 1-minute increments, stirring after each minute, until the lemon curd is thick and coats the back of a spoon.

3. Strain the curd through a fine-mesh sieve to remove any lumps. Pour the curd into the prepared crusts.

4. Make the lemon pudding according to the package directions.

5. Fold in the whipped topping.

6. Dollop each pie with the pudding–whipped topping mixture.

7. Refrigerate the pies overnight.

8. Top with lemon slices and zest. Sprinkle with sugar and slightly torch (optional).

9. Serve chilled.

NOTE

If torching the tops: Using a kitchen blow torch with a medium flame, pass over the topping on the bars, just barely above the surface, working in a circular pattern until the surface turns a light golden brown.

Cookies-and-Cream
Ice Cream Cake

Yield: 1 cake; serves 8 to 10 | Prep Time: 15 minutes | Chill Time: Overnight

My husband wanted our wedding cake to be an ice cream cake. It didn't work out, but the point is: he loves ice cream, even more than I do. I made this cake for his birthday one year, and to this day, I think he regrets not insisting on having it at our wedding.

INGREDIENTS

24 Oreo cookies

1 (8-ounce) container frozen whipped topping, thawed

9 store-bought ice cream sandwiches

DIRECTIONS

1. In the bowl of a stand mixer, mix the cookies into chunks. Set aside ⅓ cup for garnish.

2. Add in the whipped topping until well combined.

3. On a freezer-safe serving platter, place 3 of the ice cream sandwiches next to each other to form a layer. Spread with ⅓ cup of the topping-crumb mixture. Repeat with a layer of sandwiches, topping mixture, and another layer of sandwiches to make 3 layers of sandwiches. "Frost the cake" with the remaining topping-crumb mixture and sprinkle the reserved crumbs on top.

4. Wrap the cake tightly with plastic wrap and place in the freezer overnight.

5. Run a knife under hot water to slice and serve.

No-Fry Fried Ice Cream

Yield: 6 scoops | Prep Time: 30 minutes | Chill Time: 1 hour

I remember eating fried ice cream at a Mexican restaurant in Connecticut. It was always a fun way to end dinners out with girlfriends. I love recipes that deliver on a favorite food without the intricacy or challenge that the original version calls for. This no-fry ice cream tastes just like it was deep-fried but without hot oil and temperamental timing.

INGREDIENTS

6 cups cornflakes

¾ cup maple syrup

1 cup graham cracker crumbs

1 gallon vanilla ice cream, softened

1 cup chocolate sauce for serving

DIRECTIONS

1. Line a baking sheet with parchment paper.

2. In a food processor, combine the cornflakes, maple syrup, and graham cracker crumbs and process until thick and smooth.

3. Using an ice cream scoop, create a solid ball of ice cream and roll it in the coating mixture. Place on the lined baking sheet. Repeat 5 more times.

4. Freeze until ready to serve.

5. To serve, pour chocolate sauce in the bottom of six bowls and top each with an ice cream ball.

Frozen Hot Chocolate

Yield: 3 frozen hot chocolates | Prep Time: 5 minutes | Assemble Time: 10 minutes

I remember when Frozen Hot Chocolate became a big fad at a place in New York City. The restaurant, Serendipity III, featured this drink, and I wanted nothing more than to try it myself. Like any love story, where someone is meant to find another person despite all the odds, I ended up finding a way to it and have since made it at home as a reminder of the power of persistence.

INGREDIENTS

2 cups whole milk

½ cup hot cocoa mix (or two single-serving packets)

¼ cup malted milk powder

3 cups crushed ice

Whipped cream and chocolate sprinkles for garnish (optional)

DIRECTIONS

1. Combine all of the ingredients except for the whipped cream and chocolate sprinkles in blender. Blend on high until frothy.

2. Garnish with a dollop of whipped cream and chocolate sprinkles, if desired. Serve immediately.

Raspberry Sorbet

Yield: Serves 4 | Prep Time: 5 minutes | Chill Time: 4 hours

With just two ingredients, this sorbet will become your new go-to method of serving a fancy fruity frozen dessert to all of your guests, and this time you can say it is homemade!

INGREDIENTS

3 cups fresh raspberries

¼ cup sweetened condensed milk

DIRECTIONS

1. Combine the raspberries and milk in the bowl of a food processor and process until smooth.

2. Transfer to an airtight container and freeze for 4 hours.

3. Remove the sorbet from the freezer and scoop into 4 of your prettiest serving dishes. Serve.

Grasshopper Pie

Yield: 1 pie; serves 6 to 8 | Prep Time: 15 minutes | Chill Time: 4 hours

First came the Grasshopper cocktail with crème de menthe, making it green and coining the name. Sometime around the '60s, the name was handed down to a pie. I love stories like these because most people know what Grasshopper Pie is but never stop to think what a grasshopper has to do with it.

INGREDIENTS

½ (10-ounce) package Grasshopper Mint & Fudge cookies

2 (8-ounce) packages cream cheese, at room temperature

1 (14-ounce) can sweetened condensed milk

3–4 drops green food coloring

1 store-bought (or homemade) chocolate crumb crust

Chopped mint Oreos

DIRECTIONS

1. In the bowl of a food processor, pulse the cookies into fine crumbs. Reserve ¼ cup of the crumbs for garnish.

2. In the bowl of a stand mixer fitted with the paddle, beat the cream cheese until smooth. Add the condensed milk and beat until well combined and smooth, about 2 minutes, scraping down the sides and bottom of the bowl once. Add enough food coloring to achieve a light mint green color and stir in the cookie crumbs.

3. Spoon the filling into the prepared crust and smooth the top.

4. Sprinkle the reserved crumbs on top with the chopped mint Oreos and cover the pie with plastic wrap. Refrigerate for 4 hours or up to 1 day. Cut into slices and serve.

No-Churn Coffee Ice Cream

Yield: Serves 4 | Prep Time: 5 minutes | Chill Time: 6 hours

Coffee pairs well with chocolate. When these twin sources of caffeine come together, they form a beautiful combination of energy and comfort. I always delight people when I serve homemade coffee ice cream with mini chocolate chips on top.

INGREDIENTS

2 cups heavy whipping cream

1 (14-ounce) can sweetened condensed milk

1 tablespoon instant brewed espresso

2 teaspoons vanilla extract

Mini chocolate chips for garnish

DIRECTIONS

1. In the bowl of a stand mixer fitted with the wire whip, mix the heavy whipping cream until stiff peaks form.

2. Add the condensed milk, espresso, and vanilla and whip for an additional 2 minutes.

3. Freeze in an airtight container for 6 hours.

4. Scoop the ice cream and serve with mini chocolate chips.

Snickerdoodle Milk Shake

Yield: Serves 2 | Prep Time: 5 minutes | Chill Time: n/a

When I was younger, my grandfather made root beer floats after dinner. That melty vanilla ice cream combined with the sweet soda was unlike anything else. We would sit up at the kitchen bar, and it felt like our own private soda shop. This is a slightly different dessert, but it reminds me of that soda-shop feel. Toss salty and sweet treats in a blender and serve up this post-dinner treat.

INGREDIENTS

2 chocolate chip cookies

2 cups snickerdoodle ice cream

¾ cup whole milk

2 tablespoons creamy peanut butter

¼ cup salted pretzels

DIRECTIONS

1. Combine all the ingredients in a blender. Blend on high until smooth.

2. Pour and serve.

Spumoni Terrine

Yield: Serves 8 to 10 | Prep Time: 15 minutes | Chill Time: 1 hour

Spumoni was created in Sicily by the Lo Monaco family and remains popular in Italian segments of the United States today. Combining three flavors and colors of ice cream, you might call it the original sundae. My take is a spumoni terrine, layering the flavors, freezing, and then slicing it to make a cake piece. It's a different way to enjoy a scoop!

INGREDIENTS

1 pint strawberry ice cream

1 pint chocolate ice cream

1 pint pistachio ice cream

Maraschino cherries for garnish

DIRECTIONS

1. Bring the three ice cream containers out of the freezer and allow to thaw for 5 to 10 minutes.

2. Lightly coat a 9 × 5-inch loaf pan with cooking spray and line it with a piece of plastic wrap.

3. Place the pistachio ice cream on the bottom.

4. Top with the strawberry ice cream.

5. Add the chocolate ice cream on top.

6. Freeze for 1 hour. Remove and garnish with cherries.

7. Slice and serve immediately.

Fruity Ice Cream Sandwiches

Yield: 6 ice cream sandwiches | Prep Time: 15 minutes | Chill Time: 1 hour

The crunch of the chocolate graham crackers is a fun alternative to the soft cookie sandwiches you may be used to. And when you fold in fruit, you feel like you're eating a fruit cup within a delicious summer treat. Try it with berries or bananas: the options are endless.

INGREDIENTS

1 gallon vanilla ice cream

12 chocolate graham crackers

1 (16-ounce) bag frozen mixed fruits, including peaches

DIRECTIONS

1. Bring the vanilla ice cream out of freezer and allow it to thaw for 5 to 10 minutes. Line a baking sheet with parchment paper.

2. Lay out 6 chocolate graham crackers on the baking sheet.

3. Combine the ice cream with the fruit and mix well.

4. Scoop the fruity ice cream onto the chocolate crackers and top each with another chocolate cracker. Press gently to ensure the crackers don't break.

5. Freeze for 1 hour before serving.

Pineapple Whip

Yield: Serve 6 | Prep Time: 15 minutes | Chill Time: 1 hour

I made this pretty faux ice cream for my friend's shower, and it became one of my go-tos when hosting a summer soiree. It looks lovely on a dessert table, and I promise it will get consumed before it melts in that hot summer sun it resembles.

INGREDIENTS

1 (15-ounce) can crushed pineapple

1 (8-ounce) container frozen whipped topping, thawed

⅓ cup corn syrup

Yellow food coloring

DIRECTIONS

1. In the bowl of a stand mixer fitted with the wire whip, beat the pineapple, whipped topping, and corn syrup until combined.

2. Add enough yellow food coloring to achieve the color you desire, 3 to 5 drops.

3. Transfer to a freezer-safe container and freeze for 1 hour. Scoop out and serve.

No-Churn Vanilla Bean Ice Cream

Yield: Serves 6 | Prep Time: 5 minutes | Chill Time: 6 hours or overnight

Vanilla is my favorite flavor. With vanilla ice cream, vanilla cake, or vanilla frosting, you can't go wrong in my book. If you are looking for a no-churn, easy way to make ice cream from scratch, try this recipe.

INGREDIENTS

2 cups heavy whipping cream

1 (14-ounce) can sweetened condensed milk

2 teaspoons vanilla extract

1 teaspoon vanilla bean paste

Multicolored nonpareil chocolate chips and waffle cones for serving

DIRECTIONS

1. In the bowl of a stand mixer fitted with the wire whip, mix the heavy whipping cream on high until stiff peaks form.

2. In a large bowl, combine the condensed milk with the vanilla extract and vanilla bean paste.

3. Fold the whipped cream into the milk-vanilla mixture.

4. Freeze the ice cream for at least 6 hours or overnight. Scoop into bowls and decorate with the multicolored nonpareil chocolate chips and waffle cones to serve.

5

Gelatin and Pudding Desserts

Pudding and wobbly gelatin are two fun textures
that remind me of childhood desserts. They are
uniquely sweet and as cute as can be.

Chocolate Mousse

Yield: 1 quart; serves 6 to 8 | Prep Time: 15 minutes | Chill Time: 30 minutes or 1 day

People think of chocolate pudding or cake, but there is this forgotten cousin of those desserts somewhere in the middle, and that is mousse. It is easier to make than rumor may have it, and topped with any type of sprinkle or nut, it can be added to a menu in a heartbeat.

INGREDIENTS

2 cups heavy whipping cream

4 large egg yolks

3 tablespoons sugar

½ teaspoon instant espresso powder

Pinch of kosher salt

7 ounces unsweetened baking chocolate, finely chopped, or melting chocolate wafers

1 teaspoon vanilla extract

Pink sugar pearls for garnish

DIRECTIONS

1. Put 1¼ cups of the cream along with the metal bowl of a stand mixer in the refrigerator to chill. In a small heavy saucepan, cook the remaining ¾ cup of cream over medium-low heat until it registers 160°F on an instant-read thermometer; do not boil.

2. While the cream heats, whisk the egg yolks with the sugar, espresso powder, and salt until very smooth. Slowly drizzle some of the heated cream into the yolk mixture, stirring constantly, then return the yolk mixture to the cream in the saucepan and cook, stirring, until it again registers 160°F on an instant-read thermometer.

3. Meanwhile, bring 1 inch of water to a simmer in a medium saucepan. Put the chocolate in a metal or heatproof glass bowl and set over the simmering water to melt.

4. Remove the bowl from the heat, wipe the bottom of the bowl to prevent any water from getting into the chocolate, which will make it seize, and stir in the vanilla. Pour into a large clean bowl and set aside to cool for 5 minutes.

5. When the custard has cooled to lukewarm, whip the chilled cream until soft peaks form. Reserve ½ cup of the whipped cream to use for garnish. Fold the remaining cream and the chocolate mixture together gently until no white streaks remain. Spoon the mousse into small espresso cups. Garnish with the reserved whipped cream and pink sugar pearls and chill for at least 30 minutes or up to 1 day.

Custard

Yield: 6 individual custards | Prep Time: 25 minutes | Chill Time: 2 to 3 hours

It's a classic, and for good reason. Rich and elegant, this is a dessert I imagine women like Jacqueline Kennedy Onassis must have loved. I picture teatime in a big beautiful garden, making this bright white, tiny treat a pretty delight.

INGREDIENTS

2 cups whole milk

½ cup sugar

2 tablespoons cornstarch

4 large egg yolks

1 teaspoon vanilla extract

Fresh berries for garnish

DIRECTIONS

1. In a medium nonstick saucepan, whisk together the milk, sugar, and cornstarch over medium-low heat to combine. Heat gently, stirring, until you see steam and small bubbles form around the edges of the pan; do not boil. Remove from the heat and set aside.

2. In a medium bowl, whisk the egg yolks until light. Spoon about ½ cup of the hot milk mixture into the yolks while whisking constantly, then pour the yolk mixture back into the hot milk, whisking constantly. Return the mixture to the stove and cook over medium heat, stirring constantly with a rubber scraper, and scraping bottom and sides of the bowl so the mixture does not scorch, about 5 minutes or until the mixture has thickened enough to coat the rubber scraper. Stir in the vanilla.

3. Remove the pan from the heat and pour through a fine-mesh sieve to remove any lumps. Gently pour into six 6-ounce ramekins set on a baking sheet.

4. Cool to room temperature, then lightly cover with plastic wrap and chill for 2 to 3 hours. Garnish with fresh berries and serve.

Orange Dreamy Dessert

Yield: Sixteen 2-inch squares | Prep Time: 30 minutes | Chill Time: 4 hours

When my best friend and I needed a break from campus life and went to her parents' house on weekends, her godmother always made Jell-O. I can't help but smile when I think of how comforting and special this dessert was, each square our own little vacation, an oasis away from campus.

INGREDIENTS

Orange Layer

3 envelopes gelatin

½ cup cold water

½ cup boiling water

¼ cup sugar

2½ cups orange soda

4–5 ounces mandarin oranges, cut into chunks

Cream Layer

3 envelopes gelatin

½ cup cold water

½ cup boiling water

2 cups vanilla ice cream, completely melted

DIRECTIONS

Orange Layer

1. Sprinkle the gelatin over the cold water in a large bowl. Stir to dissolve and let sit for 1 minute.

2. Pour the boiling water with the sugar over the gelatin and stir for 2 minutes to ensure that the sugar has completely dissolved.

3. Pour in the orange soda and stir to combine. Pour the mixture into a 9 × 13-inch pan sprayed with cooking spray. Refrigerate for at least 4 hours, or until the gelatin is firmly set.

4. Remove the gelatin from the fridge and cut into ¼ × ½-inch rectangles. Spray an 8-inch square pan with cooking spray.

5. Place the gelatin pieces into the pan, spreading them out. Add the mandarin chunks around the gelatin pieces.

Cream Layer

6. In a large bowl, sprinkle the gelatin over the cold water. Stir and let sit for 1 minute.

7. Pour the boiling water over the gelatin and stir for 2 minutes until completely dissolved. Add the melted ice cream and stir to combine.

8. Pour the ice cream mixture over the gelatin and mandarin oranges.

9. Cover and refrigerate for 4 hours or overnight.

10. Cut into sixteen 2-inch squares and serve.

Strawberry Parfait Delight

Yield: 6 parfaits | Prep Time: 25 minutes | Chill Time: 1 hour 30 minutes

Let's party! Three layers make this sweet treat pretty as can be. Whether for a beach party or elegant evening, changing up the decorations will customize it for any occasion.

INGREDIENTS

1 (3.4-ounce) package of strawberry Jell-O

1 (8-ounce) container frozen whipped topping, thawed

Sliced strawberries for garnish

DIRECTIONS

1. Make the Jell-O according to the package instructions.

2. Pour half the Jell-O into a separate bowl and fold in 4 ounces of the whipped topping.

3. Place the untouched portion of the Jell-O on the bottom of six individual parfait glasses. Chill for 30 minutes. Top with the whipped topping–Jell-O combo and chill for 1 hour.

4. Remove from the fridge and top with the remaining whipped topping. Sprinkle the top with sliced strawberries. Serve immediately.

Rice Pudding

Yield: 8 individual puddings | Prep Time: 10 minutes | Cook Time: 30 minutes

Southern cooks have been making rice pudding for centuries. This is that familiar favorite—especially delicious when topped with the rich caramel sauce that tastes like melted praline candies. A hint of Kentucky bourbon makes it special, but if you wish, simply soak the raisins in water instead.

INGREDIENTS

⅓ cup bourbon

⅓ cup raisins

1 cup arborio or carnaroli rice

2 cups water

2 cups whole milk

¼ teaspoon salt

¾ cup sweetened condensed milk

¼ teaspoon ground cinnamon, plus extra for garnish

1 large egg, beaten well

2 teaspoons vanilla extract

Whipped topping for garnish

DIRECTIONS

1. In a small bowl, pour the bourbon over the raisins and set aside to soak while you prepare the rice mixture.

2. In a heavy medium nonstick saucepan, combine the rice, water, milk, and salt. Stirring continuously, bring the mixture to a boil over medium heat. Reduce the heat to low, cover, and cook for 20 to 25 minutes, stirring occasionally.

3. Remove the pan from the heat and stir in the sweetened condensed milk and cinnamon. Return to the heat and cook, stirring, for an additional 5 minutes.

4. Drain the raisins, reserving the soaking liquid. Remove the pan from the heat and gradually add the beaten egg, stirring continuously. Return the pan to the heat and cook the pudding, stirring, until the mixture has thickened, about an additional 3 minutes. Add the vanilla and stir to incorporate.

5. Pour the pudding into eight individual serving dishes and cool. Drizzle with the raisin soaking liquid. Top with whipped topping and cinnamon. Serve at room temperature.

VARIATION

Instead of the bourbon you can use water.

Pecan Dream

Yield: Serves 6 to 8 | Prep Time: 20 minutes | Chill Time: 3 hours

This is seriously one of the best foods I have ever made. I was trying to eat fewer sweets, but that didn't work out so well. I was shocked by the deliciousness of this dessert and proceeded to eat it every day until it was all gone. Try it and you'll see!

INGREDIENTS

1 cup pecans, chopped

½ cup graham cracker crumbs

3 tablespoons granulated sugar

3 tablespoons unsalted butter, melted

2 tablespoons evaporated milk

1 (8-ounce) package cream cheese, at room temperature

1 cup powdered sugar

3 cups thawed whipped topping

1 (5.1-ounce) package instant chocolate pudding mix

1 (11.75-ounce) jar store-bought caramel sauce

DIRECTIONS

1. Line an 8-inch square baking dish with parchment paper.

2. In the bowl of a stand mixer fitted with the paddle, combine the pecans, graham cracker crumbs, granulated sugar, butter, and evaporated milk and mix well.

3. Press the mixture into the lined baking dish to form a crust.

4. Meanwhile, in a clean bowl, combine the cream cheese, powdered sugar, and 1 cup of the whipped topping. Stir by hand with a whisk until smooth.

5. Make the chocolate pudding according to the package directions.

6. To assemble, spread the cream cheese mixture over the crust in an even layer, then spoon the caramel sauce on top. Top with the chocolate pudding in a smooth layer. Finally, spread the remaining 2 cups whipped topping over the cake and make swirls on top. Chill for at least 3 hours.

7. Scoop and serve.

Funfetti Birthday Cake Parfaits

Yield: 2 parfaits | Prep Time: 15 minutes | Cook Time: n/a

I love balloons more than many children I know do. Last year on my birthday, I came home to a house full of them because despite the fact that my husband thinks it's silly, he knows how much joy they bring me. I like blowing up small balloons and using them on a dessert table as decor. Nothing beats the helium ones hanging high on the ceiling, but balloons in every shape and size make any day a party. This cake, filled with confetti, reminds me of a happy home filled with balloons.

INGREDIENTS

1 (3.5-ounce) package instant vanilla pudding mix

8 Funfetti (sprinkle) chocolate chip cookies

1 cup thawed whipped topping

Sprinkles for garnish

DIRECTIONS

1. Make the vanilla pudding according to the package directions.

2. Crush up 6 of the cookies.

3. Place the cookie crumbs at the bottom of two wine glasses.

4. Top with pudding. Add another layer of cookie crumbs and another layer of pudding.

5. Dollop each with whipped topping, decorate with sprinkles, and garnish each serving with 1 of the remaining cookies.

VARIATION

You can add 1 ounce of rum on top of each dessert for a grown-up birthday.

Pineapple Dream Dessert

Yield: 4 individual desserts | Prep Time: 15 minutes | Chill Time: 1 hour

This reminds me of a piña colada, and when kids aren't being served, you better believe I add a little rum. My husband and I went to Mexico one year for my birthday, and memories of sitting by the pool with something that looks strikingly similar bring a smile to my face every time.

INGREDIENTS

1 (20-ounce) can crushed pineapple

1 (3.4-ounce) package instant banana pudding mix

1 (8-ounce) container frozen whipped topping, thawed

Maraschino cherries

DIRECTIONS

1. In a medium bowl, combine the crushed pineapple and banana pudding mix.

2. Stir in 1 cup of the whipped topping.

3. Spoon the mixture into four small glasses. Top with the remaining whipped topping and a cherry.

4. Refrigerate for at least 1 hour to allow the mixture to set. Serve chilled.

Slow Cooker Brownie Pudding

Yield: Serves 6 to 8 | Prep Time: 15 minutes | Cook Time: 2 to 3 hours

Drop it all in and go! This slow-cooker solution is a great way to make brownies without turning on the oven and heating up the house. But don't worry; that mouthwatering brownie smell will still fill your home.

INGREDIENTS

1 (18-ounce) box brownie mix

¼ cup semisweet chocolate chips

1 (3.9-ounce) package instant chocolate pudding mix

½ teaspoon instant espresso powder

2 cups whole milk

Ice cream and/or whipped cream for serving (optional)

DIRECTIONS

1. Lightly coat a 6-quart slow cooker with cooking spray.

2. Prepare the brownie mix according to the package directions.

3. Pour the batter into the slow cooker. Sprinkle the chocolate chips on top.

4. In a small bowl, whisk the pudding mix and espresso powder with the milk until combined.

5. Pour over the brownie mix in the slow cooker.

6. Place a piece of parchment paper or a paper towel between the slow cooker and the lid to catch the condensation.

7. Cook for 2 to 3 hours on high.

8. Start checking it after 2 hours. Watch for the edges to start pulling away from the insert. The pudding, however, will still look wet.

9. Serve warm with ice cream or whipped cream.

Addie's Tiramisu

Yield: 4 to 6 individual tiramisu | Prep Time: 15 minutes | Chill Time: 2 hours

I spend time writing menus for restaurants, and this recipe has its place on a menu at a restaurant in Los Angeles! It's a favorite for any occasion and any time of day, especially soaked in Baileys, my favorite to mix into an after-dinner drink. It's perfect to serve around the holidays!

INGREDIENTS

1 shot espresso

¼ cup plus 2 tablespoons Baileys Irish Cream

1 (8-ounce) container frozen whipped topping, thawed

½ cup mascarpone cheese

2 tablespoons sugar

1 (7-ounce) package ladyfingers

DIRECTIONS

1. Combine the shot of espresso with ¼ cup of the Baileys in a pie plate. Set aside.

2. In a medium bowl, whisk together the whipped topping and mascarpone cheese. Add the remaining 2 tablespoons of Baileys and the sugar.

3. Dip two ladyfingers into the Baileys-espresso mixture and place in the bottom of each of 4 to 6 wine glasses or ramekins. Top each with ½ cup of the whipped topping mixture and 2 of the remaining ladyfingers. Continue filling the glasses with the remaining whipped topping and ladyfingers.

4. Chill for 2 hours in the fridge before serving.

Champagne Mousse

Yield: 4 individual servings | Prep Time: 25 minutes | Chill Time: 4 hours

Champagne mousse in clear plastic coupes topped with white chocolate shavings and a little edible glitter makes for a dessert that is fit for a princess but is ready in minutes.

INGREDIENTS

4 large egg yolks

¼ cup sugar

1 cup plus 3 tablespoons champagne or sparkling white wine

1 (0.25-ounce) packet unflavored gelatin

1 (8-ounce) container frozen whipped topping, thawed

White chocolate shavings and edible glitter for garnish

DIRECTIONS

1. In a medium bowl, whisk together the egg yolks and sugar until pale and light.

2. Add 1 cup of the champagne and whisk until combined.

3. Pour the egg mixture into a saucepan and cook over medium heat, whisking constantly, until the mixture begins to thicken, 7 to 10 minutes.

4. Remove from the heat and whisk for another 1 to 2 minutes. Pour into a large bowl and set aside.

5. In a small microwave-safe bowl, sprinkle the gelatin over the remaining 3 tablespoons champagne. Set aside to dissolve.

6. Heat the gelatin-champagne mixture in the microwave for 10 to 20 seconds on high until melted.

7. Add the gelatin to the egg mixture and mix until combined.

8. Slowly fold the whipped topping into the egg mixture.

9. Spoon the mousse into four coupes, garnish with white chocolate shavings and edible glitter, and refrigerate for at least 4 hours. Serve.

6

Desserts in a Jar

Everything tastes better in a little jar! Whether
for a party or just as a grab-and-go for you, these
individual desserts are as tasty as they are cute.

Apple Pie in a Jar

Yield: Four 16-ounce jars | Prep Time: 15 minutes | Cook Time: 10 minutes

One of the things I love about apple pie is that it is an iconic dessert for two completely different holidays. I remember joining a pie-eating contest at a Fourth of July party, and when Thanksgiving comes around, I end up making something quite similar. To me, this classic American dessert is tried and true and can be eaten year-round. Put it in a jar and serve it to your guests in individual servings that are easy to hold and eat at either a summer party or while watching football on Thanksgiving Day.

INGREDIENTS

2 tablespoons unsalted butter

4 apples, peeled, cored, and diced

¼ cup sugar

Pinch of kosher salt

Pinch of ground nutmeg

8 large oatmeal raisin cookies

Vanilla ice cream

Store-bought caramel sauce

DIRECTIONS

1. In a medium skillet, melt the butter over medium-high heat. Add the apples, sugar, salt, and nutmeg. Cook until the apples are soft and a syrup forms, about 10 minutes. Remove from the heat and set aside to cool slightly.

2. Crumble half the cookies and divide equally among four Mason jars.

3. Layer the cooked apples over the cookie crumbles, dividing them equally. Crumble the remaining half of the cookies. Repeat, layering the cookie crumbles and apples one more time.

4. Top with a scoop of vanilla ice cream and a drizzle of caramel sauce. Serve immediately.

Drumstick Sundae

Yield: 1 sundae │ Prep Time: 5 minutes │ Chill Time: n/a

I love those Drumstick ice cream treats you can find in the frozen chest box at a gas station. I did my best to talk my parents into allowing me to have one when we drove out to our cabin on weekends. I now like re-creating that sweet treat but in a big jar, making it a little less messy than when we dripped it all over our hands in the car!

INGREDIENTS

2 sugar ice cream cones

3 scoops snickerdoodle ice cream

1 cup store-bought hot fudge sauce

DIRECTIONS

1. Crush 1 ice cream cone and place in the bottom of a 16-ounce Mason jar. Top with 2 scoops of ice cream. Drizzle with hot fudge sauce.

2. Add 1 more scoop of ice cream and top with an upside-down cone. Serve immediately.

Mint Chocolate Chip Cups

Yield: 2 jars | Prep Time: 15 minutes | Chill Time: 1 hour

My brother's favorite ice cream is mint chocolate chip. When I first made this dessert with crushed mint Oreos and vanilla and chocolate pudding, he said he would prefer to stick to his usual. I chilled it overnight, and upon first bite, he was a convert!

INGREDIENTS

24 mint Oreos

Mint chocolate chip ice cream

2 cups premade chocolate pudding

DIRECTIONS

1. Crush the Oreos and add about three-quarters to the bottom of each jar, lightly packing it down.

2. Top with a layer of mint chocolate chip ice cream and a layer of chocolate pudding.

3. Add the remaining Oreos on top.

4. Chill for 1 hour before serving.

Mason Jar Trifle

Yield: 1 individual trifle | Prep Time: 10 minutes | Chill Time: 2 hours

I have a very distinct memory of making my first trifle. It was Victorian Day in middle school, and each student volunteered to make or bring in things that would help bring the day together. I didn't know what a trifle was, but when I saw a picture of many ingredients stacked together, I wanted to learn how to make one. I should have known back then that I would be up for any culinary challenge (how do you get those layers to be so perfect?), and when given the opportunity to cook or bake for a crowd, I'm the first to raise my hand.

INGREDIENTS

6 ladyfingers

½ cup raspberry jam

1 cup thawed whipped topping

DIRECTIONS

1. Place 3 ladyfingers on the bottom of a 12-ounce Mason jar.

2. Add the raspberry jam.

3. Add the 3 remaining ladyfingers on top.

4. Spoon on the whipped topping to finish the trifle.

5. Place in the fridge to allow the ladyfingers to absorb the jam, about 2 hours.

Mini Pumpkin Pies

Yield: Eight 4-ounce pies │ Prep Time: 20 minutes │ Chill Time: 1 hour

This little treat is chilled and as smooth as pudding. It's a cinnamon-flavored creamy custard that will make you crave the beloved holiday pie year-round.

INGREDIENTS

1 (15-ounce) can pure pumpkin puree

⅓ cup light brown sugar, firmly packed

1 teaspoon ground cinnamon

½ teaspoon pumpkin pie spice

Pinch of ground cloves

Pinch of kosher salt

2 tablespoons heavy whipping cream

12–15 amaretti cookies, crushed

Whipped topping

DIRECTIONS

1. In a bowl, mix together the pumpkin puree, brown sugar, cinnamon, pumpkin pie spice, cloves, salt, and heavy whipping cream until well combined. Transfer to the refrigerator to chill.

2. Place the crushed amaretti cookies in the bottom of each jar. Top with the chilled pumpkin filling and a dollop of whipped topping. Serve.

Chocolate-Raspberry Cheesecake in a Jar

Yield: Four 4-ounce cheesecakes | Prep Time: 25 minutes | Chill Time: 1 hour

Chocolate-covered strawberries are a well-known indulgence, but let me tell you that raspberries dunked in dark chocolate are a best-kept secret.

INGREDIENTS

1 cup heavy whipping cream

1½ teaspoons vanilla extract

½ cup plus 3 tablespoons powdered sugar

1 (8-ounce) package cream cheese, at room temperature

¼ teaspoon instant espresso powder

3 tablespoons unsweetened cocoa powder

Pinch of kosher salt

6 chocolate cookies, crushed

1 pint fresh raspberries

DIRECTIONS

1. In the bowl of a stand mixer fitted with the wire whip, mix the heavy whipping cream on high speed until stiff peaks form. Add 1 teaspoon of the vanilla and ½ cup of the powdered sugar and whip to incorporate. Scrape the whipped cream into a separate bowl and set aside.

2. In a clean mixer bowl fitted with the paddle, whip the cream cheese, the remaining 3 tablespoons powdered sugar, espresso powder, cocoa powder, salt, and remaining ½ teaspoon vanilla on high speed until fluffy and smooth.

3. Scrape down the sides of the bowl. Add 1 cup of the whipped cream and fold in carefully until no white streaks remain.

4. Press an even layer of cookie crumbles into each Mason jar, pressing it down with the back of a spoon. Add a layer of the cheesecake mixture to each jar, filling until almost full. Top with plenty of fresh raspberries.

5. Refrigerate for 1 hour, or until set. Serve.

Strawberry Shortcake in a Jar

Yield: 2 shortcakes | Prep Time: 5 minutes | Chill Time: 1 hour

This reminds me of a tea cake that would fit in a secret garden in a childhood story. Like in any fairy tale, if you look closely, you'll find something new every time. On this little jar is an etched strawberry, right smack in the middle, but easy to miss upon first glance. It is as tiny as it looks and is the cutest treat for those who believe.

INGREDIENTS

6 mini vanilla wafer cookies

1 cup thawed whipped topping

½ cup sliced strawberries

DIRECTIONS

1. Place 3 vanilla wafer cookies on the bottom of each jar.

2. Add ¼ cup of the whipped topping to each jar.

3. Divide ¼ cup of the strawberries, the remaining ½ cup whipped topping, and the remaining ¼ cup strawberries between the two jars.

4. Chill for 1 hour before serving to allow the vanilla wafers to absorb the whipped topping.

Individual Peanut Butter Cups

Yield: 2 peanut butter cup jars | Prep Time: 15 minutes | Chill Time: n/a

Someone once told me that when feeding a dog peanut butter on a spoon you have to be careful that she won't lap that whole spoon down, and I think of that every time I try this dessert. It is easy to get carried away getting to every last bite!

INGREDIENTS

2 cups mini Reese's peanut butter cups

8 peanut butter Oreos

8-ounces cream cheese, at room temperature

½ cup powdered sugar

1 cup creamy peanut butter

DIRECTIONS

1. Place ½ cup of the mini peanut butter cups on the bottom of each jar. Add 4 crushed peanut butter Oreos on the bottom of each jar.

2. In the bowl of a stand mixer fitted with the paddle, beat the cream cheese, sugar, and peanut butter on medium speed until well combined. Add ½ cup of the peanut butter cups and the remaining 4 peanut butter Oreos and continue to beat until broken up and well distributed.

3. Spoon the cream cheese mixture on top of the peanut butter cups and crushed Oreos.

4. Top with the remaining peanut butter cups and Oreos and serve.

Vanilla Beach

Yield: Two 4-ounce jars | Prep Time: 5 minutes | Chill Time: n/a

There's always a reason to take a trip to the beach to enjoy the sunshine and pretend that your toes are touching the sand, even if you're stuck indoors. This dessert will get you there, guaranteed.

INGREDIENTS

2 (3.25-ounce) containers premade vanilla pudding

4 graham crackers, crushed

2 sour gummy octopi

Cocktail umbrellas (optional)

DIRECTIONS

1. Spoon the vanilla pudding onto the bottom of two 4-ounce jars or glasses.

2. Top each with crushed graham crackers and a sour gummy octopus.

3. Garnish each with an umbrella if you have them! Serve immediately.

S'mores in a Jar

Yield: Two 4-ounce jars | Prep Time: 5 minutes | Cook Time: n/a

When sitting around a fire pit, beach fire, or campsite, it's fun to serve and eat something that fits the theme but is prepared beforehand. If you make and serve these portable cups for your camping trip or bonfire night, people will be asking for more.

INGREDIENTS

2 (3.25-ounce) containers premade chocolate pudding

6 graham crackers, crushed

1 cup mini marshmallows

DIRECTIONS

Layer the chocolate pudding, graham cracker crumbs, and marshmallows in two 4-ounce glass jars, dividing the ingredients equally.

Dirt Cup

Yield: 8 to 10 dirt cups | Prep Time: 30 minutes | Chill Time: 30 minutes

I teach first graders about healthy eating, and recently when describing root vegetables, I explained that you are eating what is underground in the dirt. One smart kid was eager to remind me that we are not supposed to eat dirt. I asked, "What about dirt cups?" Without a doubt, the class knew what those were! As a child I ate these, and it is fun to see that kids still do. I am determined to keep the worms in and carry on the tradition.

INGREDIENTS

1 (14.3-ounce) package Oreo cookies

1 (8-ounce) package cream cheese, at room temperature

8 tablespoons (1 stick / ½ cup) unsalted butter, softened

1 cup powdered sugar

1 teaspoon vanilla extract

3 cups cold whole milk

2 (3.4-ounce) packages instant vanilla pudding mix

1 (8-ounce) container of whipped topping

Sour worms

DIRECTIONS

1. In a food processor, pulse the cookies until they look like soil.

2. In the bowl of a stand mixer fitted with the paddle, beat the cream cheese, butter, powdered sugar, and vanilla until light and fluffy.

3. In a large bowl, whisk together the milk and pudding mixes for 2 minutes until thickened.

4. Fold the whipped topping into the pudding.

5. Fold the pudding mixture into the cream cheese mixture until well combined.

6. Spoon three-quarters of the crushed cookies and filling into eight to ten 8-ounce glasses, layering along the way. Chill for 30 minutes.

7. Top with the remaining crushed cookies and garnish with sour gummy worms. Serve.

Pretzel Butterscotch

Yield: 2 jars | Prep Time: 5 minutes | Chill Time: n/a

Crushed pretzels and butterscotch chips topped with chocolate pudding and whipped topping guarantee that one spoon in, you'll be sold on the salty-sweet combo.

INGREDIENTS

2 cups salted pretzels

½ cup butterscotch chips

2 (3.25-ounce) containers premade chocolate pudding

1 cup thawed whipped topping

DIRECTIONS

1. Pour the salted pretzels into a zip-top bag, seal, and crush the pretzels with your hand or a mallet.

2. Spoon three-quarters of the crushed pretzels into the bottom of each jar, dividing them equally and reserving the remainder for garnish. Top with a few butterscotch chips.

3. Add the chocolate pudding on top of pretzels and butterscotch chips. Top with the whipped topping.

4. Garnish with the reserved pretzels and butterscotch chips and serve.

Banana Cream Pie in a Jar

Yield: Four 4-ounce jars | Prep Time: 15 minutes | Chill Time: 30 minutes

This is another one of those desserts that reminds me of the '50s. Creamy banana pudding with whipped topping could be as simple as it gets, but with vanilla wafers on the bottom and fresh slices on top, it goes above and beyond.

INGREDIENTS

1 (3.4-ounce) package instant banana pudding mix

2 cups vanilla wafer cookies, crushed

1 (8-ounce) container frozen whipped topping, thawed

1 banana, peeled and sliced for serving

DIRECTIONS

1. Make the banana pudding according to the package directions.

2. Fill the jars with the crushed vanilla wafers, about ½ cup per jar. Chill for 30 minutes.

3. Top with the pudding, then a dollop of the whipped topping, and finish with the fresh banana slices.

Acknowledgments

I went to an all-girls boarding school in Farmington, Connecticut. It sounds fancy, I know. But it wasn't about balancing plates on our heads or learning to tie a bow tie—it was about education, athletics, and friendships. I was hesitant to leave, thinking that this faraway East Coast place could never feel like home, and I was worried I wouldn't make friends. But my, was I wrong. I was homesick at first, but after a few months, Main Street became my home, and it still feels like one today.

Mrs. Ford (I still can't seem to call her by her first name, Birch) was elegant and strict, inspiring and bold. She led the school and she led us all. I met Chris and Linda Noll, who became like parents to me, and to this day still are. I found my best friend, Adriana Valenciano, who fifteen years later was my maid of honor. My opposite, as we truly are, who became my sister, my family, as did her parents, Daisy Rodriguez and Brent Edwards. Adriana and her mother, Daisy, can't seem to find enough opportunities to send me a sweet note, a beautiful gift, and most definitely would do anything for me. Her godmother, Violet Sanchez, made us Jell-O, did our laundry, and gave us a lot of love. Violet's son, Armando Sanchez, would drop anything to pick us girls up. I met a group of girls who are equally as intelligent as they are beautiful and who push me daily to be my best. Thank you to Kelly O'Brien, and to Emily Maguire and her beautiful family, Johanne, Hank, Matt, and Maggie Maguire. Thank you to Eleanor Bradley, and Mei Ling Wong, and thank you, Alice Johnson.

That best friend of mine, Adriana, and I turned a wall in our dorm room into our inspiration. We ripped out Martha Stewart magazine pages and posted them all over that wall, because at the time I wanted to be just like Martha and any magazine inspiration that would lead me closer to her felt well worth our time designing what is now called our wedding wall. Years later I began working for Martha, and that dream, to be in her amazing, brilliant presence, became a reality, one that being at Miss Porter's allowed me pursue. I met such creative and talented people like Pilar Guzman and Yolanda Edwards. I was encouraged and mentored by Joe Lagani, Alison Matz, Karen Stroble, and Vanessa Goldman Drossman. I found true friends, Kimrie Savage and Allie Donnelly.

And after leaving her company, cities and jobs later, I was over-the-moon honored to be asked to write for her. Every moment spent with Martha has inspired me to be a better host, a better cook, a better woman. I thank her for sharing such amazing opportunities with women, as we are stronger together when we encourage and support each other's dreams.

Thank you to my incredible culinary and creative team at Prime Publishing. Tom Krawczyk, my photographer and videographer. Chris Hammond, Judith Hines, and Marlene Stolfo, my culinary test kitchen geniuses. To word masters and editors Bryn Clark and Jessica Thelander. And to my amazing editor and friend, Kara Rota. This book was a team effort, filled with collaboration and creativity that reached no limits.

Index

About the Author

After receiving her master's in culinary arts at Auguste Escoffier in Avignon, France, Addie stayed in France to learn from Christian Etienne at his three-Michelin-star restaurant. Upon leaving France she spent the next several years working with restaurant groups. She worked in the kitchen for Daniel Boulud and moved coast to coast with Thomas Keller, building a career in management, restaurant openings, and brand development. She later joined Martha Stewart Living Omnimedia, where she worked with the editorial team as well as in marketing and sales. While living in New York, Addie completed her bachelor's degree in organizational behavior. Upon leaving New York, Addie joined gravitytank, an innovation consultancy in Chicago. As a culinary designer at gravitytank, Addie designed new food products for companies, large and small. She created edible prototypes for clients and research participants to taste and experience, some of which you may see in stores today. In 2015 she debuted on the Food Network, where she competed on *Cutthroat Kitchen* and won!

Addie is the executive producer for RecipeLion. Addie oversees and creates culinary content for multiple web platforms and communities, leads video strategy, and the production of in-print books. Addie is passionate about taking easy recipes and making them elegant, from fine dining to entertaining, to innovation and test kitchens.

Addie and her husband live in Lake Forest, Illinois, with their happy puppy, Paisley. Addie is actively involved with youth culinary programs in the Chicagoland area, serving on the board of a bakery and catering company that employs at-risk youth. She is a healthy-food teacher for first graders in a low-income school district, and aside from eating and entertaining with friends and family, she loves encouraging kids to be creative in the kitchen!